# Humanidad

George I. Sánchez

# Humanidad

## Essays in Honor of George I. Sánchez

Edited by

*Américo Paredes*

Monograph No. 6
Chicano Studies Center Publications
University of California, Los Angeles

LC
2682
.H916

Rosa Martinez Cruz, *Publications Coordinator*
Production, Alicia Teichman, Dora Torres

**Cover Design:** Serena Sharp for UCLA Publication Services

© 1977 by the Regents of the University of California, Chicano Studies Center. All rights reserved under Pan American and International Copyright Conventions. Printed in El Pueblo de Nuestro Señora La Riena de Los Angeles de Porciúncula, Califas, Aztlan. U.S.A.

# Sombras Antiguas

shadows darkened by age
cast sueños antiguos
    on wood fibers
    on life nerves
path of corazón
independiente líquido sagrado
bajo el sol de rayos emplumados
la tierra de capas escamadas
los pechos, nourish mazorcas encueradas
    maiz offerings
to the temple of flesh
to the temple of bones
    mortal offerings
to mortal bodies
to corazones eternos
to rostros mortales
peace exhaled by flowers in midafternoon
respeto a las carnes, huesos y sangre
ajeno a la violencia ante el derecho
respeto a lo vivo y lo muerto
propio encuentro con reflejos apagados y oscuros
paz entre los vivos en la luz
    eternal transformation
never dead and gone
    only absent flowersong

*Alurista*

# Contents

George I. Sánchez     Frontispiece

Foreword     ix

A Humanistic Approach to the Schooling of the Bilingual-Bicultural Student     1
**David Ballesteros**

A Great American     14
**Joe J. Bernal**

The Spanish Language in the Southwest     19
**Arthur L. Campa**

On Chicano History: In Memoriam, George I. Sánchez 1906–1972     41
**Jesus Chavarria**

The Humanization of Bilingual-Bicultural Schooling     58
**Ernesto Galarza**

Three Intellectuals: Justo Sierra, Trinidad Sánchez Santos, Ricardo Flores Magón     75
**Juan Gómez-Quiñones**

George Sánchez and Testing     107
**Richard E. López and Julian Samora**

George Sánchez: Teacher, Scholar, Activist     116
**Carey McWilliams**

Jorge Isidoro Sánchez y Sánchez (1906–1972)     120
**Américo Paredes**

Perspectives on the Chicano 127
Paul S. Taylor

A Bibliography of George I. Sánchez 134
James N. Mowry

About the Contributors 143

# Foreword

*Humanidad* has many meanings: mankind, human nature, human feeling, kindness, education, culture. All these things were part of George Sánchez's life as teacher, scholar, and advocate of human rights. The variety of fields professed by his colleagues and friends attest to the wide range of his activities. Those who did not know him personally were also inspired by him.

The contributors to this volume honoring George Sánchez's memory reflect the breadth of his work. They include scholars and men in public life, young Chicano activists who looked up to him as a predecessor, veterans of the education and civil rights battles of the forties and fifties, the young and the old, Mexicanos and Anglos—a fitting testimony of the legacy George Sánchez left us.

I am greatly indebted to the Chicano Studies Center Publications (UCLA) and to its editors, who recognize the value all of us place on George Sánchez's memory, and who have made it possible for this tribute to be seen in print.

Most especially, the editor thanks Dr. Luisa Sánchez, who was most helpful in giving bibliographical and other information about her late husband.

Américo Paredes

# A Humanistic Approach to the Schooling of the Bilingual-Bicultural Student

## DAVID BALLESTEROS

"... the child's vernacular, his mother tongue, is a valuable asset in any educational program that is conducted in another language."

George I. Sánchez

Bilingualism and biculturalism may be a lifelong process but needs constant reinforcement to survive. It is an experience, a way of life, that needs to be maintained from early childhood through adult life. Spanish-surnamed students upon entering school bring with them a culture, a language that ought to be developed fully along with the study of English and the other cultures that comprise this country. The school must not be an obstacle but a facilitator in seeing that students can take full advantage of their bilingual-bicultural background.

The enactment of the Bilingual Education Act gives impetus to the schooling of the Spanish-speaking student. It provides a national commitment for significant changes in the educational policy of school districts and teacher-training institutions. It gives moral and legislative recognition to the assets of a people whose mother tongue is not English. Bilingual-bicultural schooling serves five positive purposes for the student and the school: 1. It reduces "retardation" through the use of the mother tongue in teaching, thus allowing a child to learn immediately; 2. It reinforces the relations of the school and the home through a common bond; 3. It projects the individual into an atmosphere of personal identification, self-worth, and achievement; 4. It gives the student a base for success in the field of work; 5. It preserves and enriches the cultural and human resources of a people.

Bilingual schooling is the concurrent use of two languages. Bicultural schooling is the concurrent use of two ways of life, two cultural points of view. Language is an integral part of the culture. Thus, to be truly bicultural implies being bilingual. However, a person may be bilingual without being bicultural. Knowing the language of the people with whom one works does not guarantee that one understands their way of life. Cognition of a culture is not enough; it must include feeling, experience, being. Biculturalism is a state that indicates knowing and being able to operate successfully or comfortably in two cultures.

A humanistic approach to schooling is equality of opportunity for all students. It is the respect and concern for students regarding the language and culture they bring to school. It is the understanding of personal learning styles of students. It is the positive climate established for students to develop their full potential by taking advantage of their cultural and linguistic assets. It is the belief and dignity in all students regardless of race, color or creed.

## A PIONEER

Dr. George I. Sánchez, whom I consider the major exponent in bilingual-bicultural schooling among Mexican Americans, in the 1930s was promoting and analyzing the dual experiences of language and culture among the Spanish-speaking people of the Southwest. He was attacking IQ tests imposed on Mexican American students. In one of his numerous papers, "Bilingualism in the Southwest—a Tragi-Comedy," he admonishes the schools for not seizing upon Spanish as a natural cultural resource and as a means by which to bring about proficiency in the English language. Professor Sánchez viewed bilingual-bicultural schooling not only as a way to preserve our culture but also as a means for intellectual development and cultural understanding.

For over forty years Dr. Sánchez was an educator, a scholar, a spokesman. He influenced many Mexican Americans to pursue higher education and many of them presently hold key teaching and administrative positions at all levels of schooling

# AN APPROACH

throughout the United States. I was privileged in working with him at the University of Texas at Austin for two years. I can remember sitting in his office discussing the problems and assets of Chicanos, of his concern that La Raza was not advancing fast enough, of strategies on how to beat the establishment, of methods and materials most suitable for Mexican American students, of our Indian-Spanish-Mexican heritage.

Dr. George Sánchez was a fighter to the end. Using his experiences in his native state of New Mexico and his travels in other southwestern states, he began criticizing a schooling system that imposed a monolingual, monocultural curriculum on Mexican American students. In 1968, during the hearings before the U.S. Commission on Civil Rights in San Antonio, Dr. Sánchez was asked if there was any reason why bilingual classes should not be taught. His response was that there was no reason under the sun, that way back in the sixteenth century in México, people sent their children to school where three languages were taught—Spanish, Latin, and Nahuatl—without any ill effects.[1] A few months before his death, he was testifying in court against practices which segregated Chicano students.

## NEGLECT

Better schooling for Spanish-speaking students is no longer going to be a hope and a prayer but a demand. The Mexican American youth movement, which has so eloquently raised the cry, ya basta, has focused its efforts on destroying the belief that the bilingual-bicultural person is disadvantaged, handicapped. The participants are striking at the long-held debilitating syndrome that the school can teach only those whose mold fits the curriculum. They are saying that if that is the extent of the school's capacity, then truly the schools and training institutions are disadvantaged, handicapped, for they cannot cope with different manners of behavior. These schools and training institutions must change their programs to meet the students instead of trying to compensate the students for failure to meet the school. Otherwise, the lower class and minority students who do not fit the middle class mold are less likely to be schooled and more likely to become drop-out statistics.

The number of Chicano and other Spanish-speaking students who begin school in our system without knowing English runs into the hundreds of thousands. The trend has been to force these students to repeat grade levels and to postpone any serious academic work until they learn English. This latter approach commonly leaves the Spanish-speaking student three to five years behind his Anglo counterpart by the time he is a teenager.

The notion of cultural superiority has seriously harmed the image of the United States in its dealings with other nations and with minorities in this country.[2] Whereas European children grow up with the notion of cultural diversity and frequently learn two or three languages in the course of their formal schooling, students in the United States commonly are isolated from cultural exchange. This cultural isolation is reflected in the neighborhoods, in the churches, in the schools, and in club activities.

It is a striking contradiction that in this country millions of dollars are spent to encourage students to learn a second language—and Spanish is one of the popular electives—but, at the same time many school officials frown upon Chicano students speaking Spanish at school. It is easier and safer to prohibit the speaking of Spanish on the school grounds and in the classroom (the need being to learn English) than to take the imaginative step of teaching English and Spanish to both Anglo and Spanish-speaking students beginning in the elementary school. As a consequence, the "educated" Spanish-speaking person who has survived the school system is likely to be one who has been stripped of his native language, or at best, speaks and writes it imperfectly.

By the time a student is old enough to begin our public school system, much of his skill in language, much of his cultural behavior and his personality have already been developed and determined. What he finds when he gets to school will either reinforce and stimulate the learning process he has begun or else bring such trauma that his intellectual growth will be stunted. The different ways students perceive and react to their worlds must be observed and understood as precisely as possible if teaching is to meet the student where he is at so as to maximize his development. Educability, for linguistically and culturally distinct students, should be defined primarily as the ability to learn new cultural patterns within the experience base and the culture with which the student is already familiar.

Shortly after entering primary grade, the Mexican American child begins to realize that he is different and that his difference is taken by society at large as a sign of inferiority. It is not only his schoolmates who teach him this; frequently the teachers

# AN APPROACH

themselves betray an ill-disguised contempt for the schools and neighborhoods in which they work. The opinions of the teachers are reinforced by history books, in which the youngsters read of the Spanish Inquisition, of Mexican bandits, of the massacre at the Alamo. The result of this kind of teaching—or lack of teaching—by both school and society is that the Chicano student is kept ignorant of the significant contributions his forebears made towards developing this land, nuestra tierra. At a time when he should be developing pride in his history and his own unique kind of "Americanism," he is made to feel that he does not have a right to participate in the U.S. enterprise, that he is an intruder in his own land.

A large percentage of Chicano students are still isolated in schools that are predominantly Chicano, a situation caused by de facto segregation or gerrymandered school boundaries. While the segregated Anglo-American students are equally deprived of a heterogeneous environment that could lead to increased development, they are rarely confronted with a school environment which directly rejects the culture of their home environment: lifestyles, food, family relationships, holidays, and even physical appearance.

The use of achievement tests or aptitude tests for selecting and sorting out students has persisted through the ages and remains unquestionably most prevalent in our public school system today. The widespread use of tests for purposes of selection, for deciding from kindergarten on up who will succeed and who will fail, is endemic to the kind of competitive culture that characterizes all our social institutions.

The full potential of an individual's contribution to society is sacrificed when he is denied adequate opportunities. Failure to consider both the values as well as the handicaps of bilingualism and placement of a large number of bilingual students in remedial and special education classes are examples of discrimination against Mexican American students. Poor teaching cannot be justified on the assumption that the student cannot learn. Disproportionate numbers of Spanish-speaking students are placed in classes for the mentally retarded because they cannot cope with the placement tests given in English. Many are also forced into remedial and non-academic subjects. Frustrated and misunderstood, Spanish-speaking students are rushed through or pushed out. A major cause of the high drop-out rate is the general discouragement and low morale of minority students caused by the treatment they receive in school. When the student begins to discover that the teacher does not understand him, he develops negative reactions not only to the teacher but to the schooling process and finally to the entire culture and language the teacher represents.

Teacher-preparation institutions have done and continue to do little to aid their students in coping with the problems and assets of minority students. Colleges and universities continue to certify teachers who will have life-long contact with students from different ethnic backgrounds, but do little or nothing to specifically prepare them. There are few special courses or sequences intended to provide future elementary and secondary teachers with either the skills or the understanding of linguistically and culturally distinct students.

Why isn't the bilingual-bicultural student prepared to attend and remain in institutions of higher learning? The reasons in the main are that our school system is not geared to meet the needs of Spanish-speaking students, thus developing an atmosphere of discouragement. The Spanish-surname college population is very small, fewer yet are the college graduates. In California, for example, which boasts a large college population, blacks and Chicanos make up 18.3% of the state population, yet constitute only 3.8% of the students in universities, 5.8% of the state colleges, and 11% of community colleges.[3]

The Spanish-speaking community needs more college graduates. The importance of graduating cannot be taken lightly. One of the most important routes by which the Mexican American may reach some measure of equal opportunity with other citizens is schooling. For every successful man or woman of Mexican descent, there will be innumerable others who will be inspired and motivated to move ahead.

## IDENTITY

Chicano students can learn. Their language and culture should not be obstacles to their success in school but effective tools for learning. To destroy their language and culture is to destroy their identity, self-image, and self-esteem. To survive in our monolingual-monocultural society they must be able to put into that society an extra ingredient—one that marks them as persons with a valuable asset for the enrichment of the total society. That extra ingredient is their linguistic, cultural, and ethnic pride.

# AN APPROACH

The word Chicano is an authentic expression of self-identity among us; it is a word of dignity, self-awareness, survival, brotherhood or carnalismo, that is used within our own social world—la colonia, el barrio, or the extended Chicano community.

We Chicanos have roots in América. Our Indian-Spanish ancestors were here before the Pilgrims landed at Plymouth Rock in 1620. Our present native language was the first European language spoken in América; yet Mayan and Aztec architecture was at its zenith long before Cortés landed in México in 1519. The University of México was established in 1542, nearly 100 years before Harvard. Aztlán, the Aztec word for northwest México, is the spiritual name among Chicanos for the Southwest. Our culture is still alive—only political boundaries have changed. Pride, dignity, concern, and feelings exist, especially among our youth who are struggling for self-identity and a positive image recognition.

> Who am I? asks a Mexican American high school student. I am a product of you and my ancestors. We came to California long before the Pilgrims landed on Plymouth Rock. We settled California, the southwestern part of the United States including the states of Arizona, New Mexico, Colorado and Texas. We built the missions, we cultivated the ranches. We were at the Alamo in Texas, both inside and outside. You know we owned California—that is, until gold was found here. Who am I? I am a human being. I have the same hope that you do, the same fears, the same drives, same desires, same concerns, same abilities; and I want the same chance that you have to be an individual. Who am I? In reality I am who you want me to be.[4]

## AN INSTRUCTIONAL PLAN

The demand for a relevant schooling experience is one of the most important features of the contemporary Chicano cultural renaissance. On high school and college campuses the demands for a relevant cultural experience has taken the form of proposals for Chicano Studies. A Chicano Studies curriculum organizes the Chicano experience, past, and present, in accordance with established cultural categories. The unity of Chicano-being is based, in large part, on the Chicano heritage, la herencia del ser Chicano.[5] This contributes to the shaping of an individual Chicano's personality through living or experiencing the Chicano culture, which in turn produces a sense of community. Thus, in Chicano

Studies, formal study is designed to influence the student's personal experience or identity and by so doing reveal to him, either by showing him or eliciting from him, the diverse aspects of himself and his community. In meeting the instructional needs of bilingual-bicultural students, both in the public schools and institutions of higher learning, standards must be reassessed regarding achievement and IQ tests, admission and academic requirements, and teaching competencies for both preservice and inservice teachers. We must look at standards in terms of diverse ethnic groups, in terms of the changing times. We do not need fewer standards but better standards. To require that a teacher know the language and cultural background of the students is indeed a very high standard, which will create a better teaching-training environment. The content of the curriculum and the teaching strategies used should be tailored to the unique learning and incentive-motivational styles of Spanish-speaking students.

It is most important that professional as well as paraprofessional personnel understand and recognize the unique cultural and linguistic differences among bilingual-bicultural students. We need competent, proficient teachers to teach our students. Let us not equate certification with being properly qualified; certified teachers are not necessarily qualified teachers. In addition to the content areas—including a knowledge of Spanish—techniques and methodologies, education curriculum, and educational psychology should include special sections of ethnic interest to allow preservice and inservice teachers to delve into cultural differences affecting classroom practices and teacher-student interaction.

An example of a sound teacher training program is the Teacher Corps project at the University of Texas at Austin.[6] Instructional staff, corpsmen, and community are working together to develop goals, objectives, and criteria for the various project components. The general objectives are geared to better prepare the teacher to do an effective job with bilingual-bicultural students:

1. The teacher will come to understand his own attitudes, anxieties, insecurities, and prejudices through a program of sensitivity development.
2. The teacher will understand the nature of the student's environment and culture (including language) through a program of teacher-interaction in the school and community.
3. The teacher will become knowledgeable of and competent in effective teaching skills and techniques.

## AN APPROACH

Objectives are designed to relate specifically to teacher understanding, attitudes, and skills which presumably will enable the teacher to provide an effective teacher-learning environment in the school. For the teacher candidate, "to strive toward understanding and respect of the child's cultural setting," specific objectives have been set:

1. To identify basic variables which comprise a cultural milieu (e.g., values, religion, customs).
2. To describe and compare effects of basic cultural variables on learning.
3. To identify effects of socioeconomic status on the student's development (physical, mental, attitudinal, social-emotional).
4. To identify pressures and expectancies of the dominant culture as they shape the student's learning experiences.
5. To identify his own stereotypes of different groups.
6. To incorporate in the instructional environment activities and materials related to the native culture of students.
7. To respond to the students in such a way that participation in these activities is encouraged.
8. To accept the student's language patterns as the starting point for communication and instruction.

Another example of a successful teacher-training program was the Mexican American Education Project at California State University, Sacramento.[7] The project had three components: early childhood education, prospective teacher fellowship, and experienced teacher fellowship. The Mexican American Education Project was one of the few efforts in the nation proposing to train teachers to develop skills and understanding and provide knowledge to stimulate alternatives to past patterns within our public schools. The program proposed to institutionally change the university in building bilingual-bicultural teacher-training delivery capability. It was to build and develop community accountability into a program proposing to service a Mexican American population. The program received national recognition and praise in serving as a model for training bilingual-bicultural teachers and schooling change-agents.

The new campus of the University of Texas at San Antonio has placed the Division of Teacher Education in the College of Multidisciplinary Studies. The emphasis will be for the teacher to obtain a wide range of experiences outside the field, in particular as it relates to cross-cultural experiences. Teachers will be prepared to work in urban settings and in the process obtain a linguistic and cultural understanding of black and Chicano students.

The sixth and final report of the Mexican American Education Study, U.S. Commission on Civil Rights, "Toward Quality Education for Mexican Americans," February 1974, recommends action at various governmental and school levels which, if implemented, will provide schooling opportunities and schooling successes for Chicano students. It is an instructional plan geared to the needs and assets of bilingual-bicultural students of the Southwest.

## COMMUNITY

An effective bilingual-bicultural program is characterized by community participation. The communiuty must be involved in the planning and implementation of any program. The community should be involved in the training of staff and should participate in classroom activities. Otherwise, we are destined to failure because the participants may not be aware of the necessity and relevance of the program in question. Communities in the past have not been involved in the planning and execution of their own programs. The community must recommend many of the elements of the program, and the community must become the main resource for the school, including participating in the evaluation process. There is no substitute for the personal communication between the home and the school; it is vital if bilingual-bicultural programs are to succeed. We must continue to encourage parents to participate in all phases of programs which affect their children.

Parent participation is particularly indispensable in bilingual-bicultural programs. In most Spanish-speaking communities, parents have a considerable knowledge of the language and heritage. Curriculum should be developed in such a way that parents can teach portions of it to their children at home. The Spanish-speaking parent will support the goals and values of the school when the school begins to recognize the worth of his culture and realizes that he can make a unique contribution.[8]

The Spanish-speaking population views the community not only as a physical setting but also as a spiritual experience—an extension of the immediate family. Whether we live in the barrio or not, we are concerned for the welfare and schooling of

# AN APPROACH

Chicano students. We as educators depend on support from the community as the community depends on our support. The pursuit of academic excellence is fully compatible with service to the community. The schooling institution is or should be, an integral part of the community and must exist primarily to serve and support it.

## SUMMARY AND CONCLUSION

The need for recognizing the bilingual-bicultural student as a positive force in our society is beyond question. Demands by Chicano students for a better schooling and a more meaningful experience in school is a noble effort. Both schools and teacher-preparation institutions must change before any real benefit will trickle down to our ultimate clients, nuestros hijos. The comitment to alleviate curriculum deficiencies in school programs from preschool through university levels must continue and must be intensified during the decade of the seventies. There is no room for deprived, disadvantaged, and handicapped students in U.S. schooling regardless of color or ethnic background.

I would like to summarize by listing and commenting on certain points that I feel are germane in humanizing the construction for bilingual-bicultural students:

1. Encourage students, make them feel proud of what they are—they should be able to succeed without losing their identity.
2. Provide services to the community; articulate with parents—unless parents and school personnel become aware of each others' values and respect these values, conflicts will continue, with the students suffering the consequences.
3. Facilitate cultural awareness sessions for school personnel—teachers, counselors, administrators.
4. Form a coalition with other ethnic groups on campus to promote needs and desires of minority students.
5. Hire and prepare staff who understand and empathize with students.
6. Reassess standards; they do not have to be lowered—most standards were made for middle class Anglo-America.
7. Seek research funds to make studies on personal characteristics of Chicano students, particularly their attitudes, values, and feelings toward teachers, subjects, parents, Anglo and other minority students, and to each other.
8. Promote legislation prohibiting discrimination against bilingual students in the testing and placing of such students in "tracks," special

education or remedial programs on the basis of factors that do not take into account their language and culture.
9. Make available in Spanish, as well as in English, notices, booklets, and other parental correspondence.
10. Promote cultural democracy; make it clear that all minority groups have made a contribution and that this country was built by many different ethnic groups.

I feel strongly that as more Chicano students are admitted into colleges and universities, more teachers are training to work in bilingual-bicultural programs, and more Spanish-speaking staff are hired in institutions of higher learning all will gain from this cross-cultural exchange, leading to a better understanding of ourselves as a multicultural nation. The Hispanic world has a legacy of humanism, the concern for man, the dignity of man, faith in mankind, belief in equality. We see this in men like Bartolomé de las Casas, the great Dominican friar who defended the Indian during the Conquest; Simón Bolívar, the Venezuelan, who gained freedom for his people; Benito Juárez, the Mexican, who believed in the respect for man, El respeto al derecho ajeno es la paz; José Martí, the Cuban, who fought for racial equality; Eugenio María de Hostos, the Puerto Rican, who through his efforts in education developed in his countrymen a new dignity. With more bilingual-bicultural instructors, students, and administrators in our institutions, I believe schooling will follow a more humanistic path that will benefit all students—both monolinguals and bilinguals.

Finally, I would like to stress the necessity of supporting schooling services that will consider the whole student, along with the needs and understanding of his family, community, and cultural and linguistic background. We must take a positive approach to see that programs are designed to make students succeed, not fail, that programs include students, not exclude them. George I. Sánchez saw bilingual-bicultural schooling as a great asset, not only in our relations with the rest of the world and our fellow citizens, but as of incalculable worth in the enhancement of the human spirit, un verdadero sentido de Raza.

### NOTES

1. Hearing before the United States Commission on Civil Rights, San Antonio, Texas, December 9-14, 1968, (Washington, D.C.: U.S. Government Printing Office), p. 95.

2. David Ballesteros, "The Foreign Language Teacher and Bilingualism," in *Hispania*, 52, 4 (1969), p. 877.

3. Harry Kitano and Dorothy Miller, *An Assessment of Educational Opportunity Programs in California Higher Education*, cited in Thomas Cottle, Jr., "Run to Freedom—Chicanos and Higher Education," *Change* (1972).

4. Henry Sioux Johnson and William J. Hernández-M., quoted in *Educating the Mexican Americans*, (Pennsylvania: Judson Press, 1970), pp. 17, 19.

5. See *El Plan de Santa Bárbara—A Chicano Plan for Higher Education*, (Santa Bárbara, California: La Causa Publications, 1970), pp. 93-103.

6. Cycle VII, Teacher Corps Proposal, University of Texas, Austin/Edgewood School District, San Antonio, November, 1971.

7. Mexican American Education Project Final Report, 1974, California State University, Sacramento.

8. Manuel Ramírez II, "Cultural Democracy: A New Philosophy for Educating the Mexican American Child," *The National Elementary Principal*, 50, 2 (November, 1970), pp. 45-46.

# A Great American

## JOE J. BERNAL

At the outset, I want to commend this group not only for conducting a meeting of this type, devoted to Human Resources and Leadership, but above all for your efforts in dedicating your conference to the late, great Dr. George I. Sánchez. Your choice of a dedication could not have been more appropriate, for no one personified a human resource for all of us in this vital area of civil rights, minority rights, and discrimination more than he, and no one in the Southwest provided more sustained leadership in the cause of Mexican Americans than he.

Many voices have been heard in this last decade or so, speaking out to protest the plight of the Mexican American in the Southwest, but George Sánchez spoke out fearlessly more than three decades ago, when his voice was the only one crying in the wilderness for this worthy cause. His task was a lonely one, speaking out against segregation and for better educational opportunities at a time when it was highly unpopular to do so in our society; yet, his words were listened to with respect because of the high-level manner of his criticism and because insistence on such things as the need for bilingual education fell at first not upon deaf but upon resisting ears. He persistently hammered away on this and other themes until the opposition discovered

---

A version of this paper was read at a Human Resources and Leadership Conference at the University of Texas, Austin, in June 1972. Mr. Bernal's remarks were also read into the record of the Texas state legislature on June 27, 1972, as Senate Concurrent Resolution No. 15, adopted by both the Senate and the House "in memory of Dr. George I. Sánchez, distinguished educator, father of Mexican American studies, intellectual leader of the Mexican American movement in Texas and the Southwest, and servant of the citizens of the State of Texas and of the United States of America."

# A GREAT AMERICAN

the truth. Many of the things that he labored for so long came true, thank God, in his own lifetime.

For the benefit of those of you who may not have had the good fortune to know Dr. Sánchez personally, let me recount for you the distinguished background of this man.

Jorge Isidoro Sánchez y Sánchez was born in Albuquerque, New Mexico, in 1906 and spoke proudly both of his Spanish-American heritage and of the fact that his ancestors were early seventeenth century colonists in New Mexico. He grew up in a rough frontier mining town, and at age seventeen began his teaching career in a one-room school in the mountains of New Mexico. He served seven years as teacher and principal, earning his B.A. degree at the same time, from the University of New Mexico, in Education and Spanish, in 1930. From 1930 to 1935, with time out for further study, he directed the Division of Information and Statistics of the New Mexico State Department of Education. In 1931 he earned his M.S. in Education at the University of Texas at Austin, and in 1934 the Ed.D. in Educational Administration, from the University of California at Berkeley.

He was a bright, hard-working, ambitious man and was aided financially in obtaining his last two degrees by fellowships from the General Education Board, a Rockefeller-endowed foundation. This led to considerable experience with education foundations. For two years, 1935-37, he was research associate of the Julius Rosenwald Fund of Chicago and did surveys of rural schools in México as well as of black southern schools in the U.S. In 1937-38, he was in Venezuela as chief consultant to the Ministry of Education, directing the newly established National Pedagogical Institute in Caracas. From 1938 to 1940, he was research associate and associate professor of education at the University of New Mexico, working with the National Youth Administration and surveying the schools of Taos County on a Carnegie grant.

His association with the University of Texas and with the state began in 1940, when he came to Austin as professor of Latin American education. He succeeded to the chairmanship of his department in 1951, but after eight years of service in that capacity he returned to fulltime research and teaching in 1959.

His lengthy career of some thirty-two years at the University of Texas was punctuated by frequent interruptions to accept important government assignments. He was on leave in 1943-44 as education specialist for the Office of the Coordinator of Inter-American Affairs. In 1947, he worked for the U.S. Bureau of Indian Affairs, surveying Navajo Indian education problems on reservations in Arizona, Utah, and New Mexico, and he described their plight in his book *The Together People* (1948). He was named to the Peace Corps Board of Directors in 1961, and also returned to Venezuela to study new Latin American school policies for the U.S. Office of Education. May of 1962 found him in Peru, representing the U.S. Agency for International Development.

George Sánchez was not only an outstanding educator and "resource person" for this nation's government, he was also an active leader in Mexican American affairs. He was a founder and president in 1941–42 of Political Association of Spanish-Speaking Organizations (PASSO), as well as of the Southwest Council on the Education of Spanish-Speaking People, of which he was president from 1945 until his death. He spoke out unceasingly against the injustice and ignorance displayed toward Spanish-Americans. He started fighting many years ago for the idea that Spanish-speaking children should be taught bilingually in the schools of Texas and other southwestern states, all of which is now accepted practice. He insisted that teachers who spoke only English misunderstood children when they talked or laughed in Spanish and mistakenly believed they were ridiculed. This ignorance, he reasoned, was the main thing behind the "speak English only" rule in many Texas schools. What young Chicano activists are protesting today are the same things George Sánchez protested in the thirties and forties, when it took even more courage to speak out.

In 1960, Sánchez served on President-elect John F. Kennedy's Citizens Committee for a New Frontier Policy in the Americas, together with such intellectuals as Averell Harriman, Adlai Stevenson, Wayne Morse, Arthur Schlesinger, Jr., and Judge Salinas of Laredo. In a position paper to that group he urged the United States to realign its policy toward the Latin American masses and work with the pensadores of Latin America such as Puerto Rico's Luis Muños Marín, rather than with reactionary politicians and the wealthy. He argued that our aid had made the rich richer and the powerful more powerful in Latin America.

Turning his attention to Latin Americans in the U.S., he said,

> We must let Latin America know that we prize their language and that we recognize our heritage from them. We can't get away with

protestation of our friendship for Latin Americans across the border when Latin Americans across the tracks in the U.S. are the most neglected minority group in this country.

Charges such as this against Texas political leaders made Dr. Sánchez a controversial figure and led to retaliation against him. He told associates that he was the lowest-paid professor at the University of Texas, but that it was a small price to pay for speaking truth to abusive power. As late as eight months prior to his death, he was still speaking out fearlessly, testifying in a Dallas court on a school segregation case before a U.S. district judge. Dr. Sánchez insisted that the segregation problem lay with the schools, not with the Mexican American child, that bilingual education should embrace all Texas school children, and that the state of Texas supported segregation of Mexican American children by a combination of teacher certification, textbook policies, and financial aid.

He criticized both the public school curriculum and the preparation of teachers in Texas colleges and universities, saying they were best suited to Eastern or Midwestern schools. Bilingual classes in the lower grades, he urged, would help the Mexican American child by not forcing him to think only in the unfamiliar language of English. The real problem, he often said, is that Texas teachers are not required to be fluent in both Spanish and English, and that they are ignorant of Texas culture. Dr. Sánchez straight-talked with everyone including young Mexican American militants. He spoke in Spanish at an "anti-gringo" meeting of young Chicanos in Austin in April, 1969, welcoming them to the University of Texas campus and took honest exception with them on several of their positions.

To sum up, then, what was Dr. George Sánchez? He was, first and foremost, an outstanding teacher and a renowned scholar whose list of publications is extensive. He was also an ardent civil rights advocate, a militant and outspoken anti-segregationist. He appeared at hearings on desegregation, calling for a system of public schools which discriminates against neither blacks nor Mexican Americans, a system which would make possible first class education in public schools without regard for ethnic or national background or culture. Dr. Sánchez was an author who wrote widely in his field of education. Even in his last years he was much in demand as public speaker and lecturer. He was the intellectual leader of the Mexican American movement in Texas and the Southwest, and he is the father of Mexican American studies, an area in which he was far ahead of his time.

To me personally, Dr. Sánchez represented a person I held in great admiration. I had heard of him during my "waking-up" years upon my return from the service in 1945. I read his books, and my admiration grew deeper. Soon I registered at the University of Texas for what was yet to come—my Ph.D. in Education—and Dr. Sánchez became my adviser. I was to know him better, and my admiration for him grew even more.

He took pride in being blackballed by Texas Education Agency (TEA) bureaucrats—for he was effective.

He was a critic—a critic of the establishment—of the Frank Erwin types.

He knew what was wrong and tried to correct it.

He loved and he hated—but he loved the right and just and hated the vain and the wrong.

He knew where the jugular vein was on the issues, and that's what he went after.

He was persistent, consistent, and always true to the mark.

He suffered pain quietly.

He was my leader.

He had self-respect and was respected.

He set an excellent example. If all of us were to be but a bit of what he was, this world would be a much better place for all of us.

He was, in short, a great American; and you do right to honor him by dedicating this conference in his honor and memory.

# The Spanish Language in the Southwest

## ARTHUR L. CAMPA

The development of the Spanish language in the Southwest reflects the history of the people who have spoken it since its introduction by the Spaniards at the end of the sixteenth century. The language spoken by the colonials then was virtually the same as the one spoken in Spain, and not much different from that of other colonists in Latin America. Like all languages of the Western world, Spanish maintained standards of usage through its written literature and also developed a language of the hearth among those who relied entirely on oral transmission because of their inability to read and write. Both levels of Spanish coexisted and filled the varied needs of all sectors of society. As time wore on, folk Spanish and the language spoken by the educated classes developed differences in pronunciation along phonetic lines common to the language. Professor Aurelio M. Espinosa made a complete study of the morphological and phonetic changes in New Mexican Spanish in 1909 which apply today as much as they did then.[1] The changes that occurred in the language of colonial literate society are developmental, while those occurring in the oral language of the folk were a form of deterioration brought about by a relaxed pronunciation and by a limited familiarity with the written word. The folk's inability to read and write led them also to preserve many forms which were current in the seventeenth century and which today are considered archaic or obsolescent. The current use of some of these archaic words among southwestern folk gives a charming historical flavor to the language, but it doesn't mean that the people today speak the language of Cervantes.

A small number of crown representatives, administrators, public functionaries, and churchmen in the principal cities of the Southwest such as Santa Fe, El Paso, and San Antonio were familiar with the language of the folk, but their duties also required them to use the more formalized language when attending to official dispatches, documents, contracts, and all legal matters connected with their offices. This type of language was less subject to change because it consisted for the most part of formulae, some of which are still current in the Spanish speaking world. The language spoken by the educated criollos and by administrators was not static, however, and continued to develop along linguistic lines until it was replaced by English. The folk who lived outside of this small cultured circle did not keep pace with the normal language changes which occurred over the past three hundred years. They continued their brand of popular speech and preserved unchanged expressions now considered obsolete, and at the same time developed the apocopations, elisions, and syllabic inversions which in linguistics are referred to as ellipsis, metathesis and epenthesis. Eventually, as the Hispanos merged into one class, the spoken Spanish became uniform, and the differences between cultivated Spanish and folk speech were erased. What is commonly heard today among the residents in the Southwest is traditional folk language together with Anglicisms, literal translations, and accretions from artificial sources such as Pachuco and what in Spanish is labelled *jerga callejera* or street slang. Ironically enough, a truer Spanish may be found in the isolated villages and in remote mountain valleys in New Mexico than in the cities where Spanish is taught in the public schools. The older Hispanos are more likely to greet a stranger by asking, "Where does your grace come from?" when they say "¿De 'onde viene su mercé?" They may drop the "d" in *dónde* and the final one in *merced* but these are normal changes which occur in folk speech throughout the Spanish speaking world.

The bulk of the population in the Southwest consisted until recently of pastoral folk, mestizos and Hispanicized Indians who relied entirely on orally learned speech because they lacked, with few exceptions, the basic skills of reading and writing. As they were introduced to the English language, they Hispanicized unfamiliar words and extended this habit to everyday Spanish idiom. Words like "park," "flunk" and "brake" were not common in Spanish days, so they simply converted them into *parquear*, *flunquear*, and *breca*. In other cases they transferred words which in Spanish were used in comparable situations such as *arrear* for "to drive." The word *arrear* is a standard Spanish word except that it is used in driving cattle and horses. The modern word in Spanish is *dirigir*. Another form of Anglicization is the literal translation of expressions from the English such as *aplicar* for "to apply" and the corresponding noun *aplicación* for "application." In Spanish one "applies" a compress, and *aplicación* means "laboriousness." The standard Spanish rendition is *solicitar* when applying for a job, and *solicitud* for application. Spanish began to deteriorate gradually as it ceased to be the language of commerce, industry, and public administration. The mandatory translations into Spanish of legislative proceedings in New Mexico, Colorado, and California helped to Anglicize the Spanish language. On the surface it seemed that both languages were on a par with each other but in reality they were not because English was the base on which the Spanish renditions were molded. Gradually, as the Spanish speaking improved their English, the use and quality of Spanish began to diminish proportionately until it became a familial tongue used for interpersonal relations, among friends and in the household. The diminishing quality of the Spanish language can be observed in the translations made in the New Mexican legislature. The earlier translations were made in standard Spanish with occasional Anglicisms, but these increased progressively as translators and interpreters became more familiar with English and less with Spanish.

The substitution of English for Spanish at home and publicly gradually pushed the Spanish language into the background. This is not unique in the Southwest; the same occurred with the German of Pennsylvania, the Italian of New York, and the French of Louisiana. It is very difficult for people to become bilingual when they are surrounded by a unicultural society, unless a very special effort is made by those who wish to preserve their own language at the same level of proficiency of the dominant tongue. Bilingualism means, in effect, biculturalism as well.

There are many factors which have been instrumental in preserving the use of the Spanish language despite all the derivations that characterize it today. First and foremost, the proximity of Mexico and the constant traffic of people coming and going has kept the language alive. Mexicans unable to speak English have to communicate with the Spanish speakers on this side of the border until they too fall in line before long and adopt the "Spanglish" of southwestern Hispanos. Moreover, these recent arrivals contribute additional words to the language and help keep it current. In spite of the limitations imposed upon the use of

Spanish by circumstance or by design, it continued to be used by Hispanos after the American occupation. In regions of the Southwest where the Anglo-Americans were a decided minority, the tables were turned and the Anglos learned Spanish in order to communicate with their friends and neighbors.

Another factor instrumental in the preservation of the Spanish language was the church, particularly when Mexican or Spanish priests were assigned to the missions. The close association of the village priests with the inhabitants provided them with oral Spanish which otherwise they would not learn. Some of the more concerned padres provided instruction in the language to the young. One well-known priest who worked diligently to provide schooling for the children of Taos was an independent priest named Martínez, who published a few issues of a newspaper in Taos called *El Crepúsculo*. It has been written that the printing press used by "El Padre Martínez" to publish his newspaper was brought to the Southwest by merchant-historian Josiah Gregg. Actually it was Antonio Barreiro who brought the press from Mexico City, sold it to Ramón Abreu, who in turn passed it on to Padre Martínez in Taos.

Shortly after the American occupation, Bishop John B. Lamy, a clergyman of French extraction, was assigned to Santa Fe. One of his main concerns was the strengthening of the educational system in the state. He brought along a number of French priests under his jurisdiction to help him revamp the church work, but their main interest lay in the establishment of educational institutions. Spanish was an incidental subject in the curriculum. Although these new padres spoke Spanish they did not have the natural fluency of those who spoke the language natively. The schools founded by Lamy, such as the free school in Santa Fe established the same year he arrived, emphasized teaching English in a curriculum designed to meet the future needs of Hispanos now living in an Anglo-American nation. Less than fifteen years after the arrival of Bishop Lamy, the foundation of Catholic schools had been firmly laid with a thriving Loretto Academy for girls and St. Michael College in Santa Fe. Another Jesuit college was built in Las Vegas, New Mexico in 1877, where instruction was given in English and Spanish. The extensive school work initiated and directed by Bishop Lamy was not designed to teach Spanish to the New Mexicans, but it did serve as a transition from Spanish to English for many new citizens under circumstances that were more favorably accepted by a predominantly Catholic population.

One year after the American occupation, Protestant church schools opened in New Mexico, led by the Baptists who established the first school in Santa Fe in 1849. After the Civil War, both the Presbyterians and the Methodists built schools in Santa Fe and in Albuquerque. Some of these institutions have continued as boarding schools to the present. The Protestant schools also emphasized an English curriculum and tried to bridge Spanish and Anglo-American culture. Spanish was included in the course of study with a view to preparing some of the young men for the ministry. Since the congregations they would serve were Spanish-speaking, it was necessary for these future ministers to improve their public speaking proficiency in the language. Both Protestant and Catholic churches have conducted services in Spanish throughout the Southwest so that indirectly those who attended services during the week were exposed to a more formal version of the language than they used at home. Other activities supervised by the churches during the Christmas season and other holidays gave the parishioners and the congregations an opportunity to use Spanish freely.

The publication of newspapers in Spanish from Colorado to California and all along the Mexican border was another means by which the Spanish language continued to live with a fluency that oral transmission alone could not have provided. More than five hundred newspapers have been published over the past one hundred twenty-five years, beginning with a periodical which Antonio Barreiro published in 1834 when he imported a printing press from Mexico. Many of these newspapers had a very short life, but there was always another paper started to replace the one that terminated. *El Crepúsculo* in Taos published a few issues in 1835, but the people in that village still remember their first newspaper. *El Nuevo Mexicano* in Santa Fe had the longest life of any newspaper published in Spanish in the Southwest. It continued with the same masthead from 1849 until 1965, and during the time it was owned by Cyrus McCormick, he made a definite attempt to upgrade the quality of the language and the content by employing an able editor from Chihuahua. Members of the Spanish faculty of the University of New Mexico and other state institutions were employed as contributors and feature writers. Many of the leading citizens of Santa Fe were also asked to contribute regularly, and for a number of years the traditional lore of the Hispanos was featured in every weekly issue.

Although many newspapers were short-lived, they provided an outlet for literary expression of Hispanos interested in writing. The names of various newspapers are in some cases indicative of their objectives and editorial policy. Such newspapers as *El Defensor del Pueblo* published in 1882 in Albuquerque alongside of *Opinión Pública* and *Nuevo Mundo* clearly indicate their mission. In the early nineteen hundreds there appeared *El Independiente* in Las Vegas, New Mexico, *La Vía Industrial* in the non-industrial town of Antonio, Colorado; *La Opinión Pública* in Walsenburg, Colorado; *El Heraldo del Valle* in Las Cruces, New Mexico; *La Revista* in Taos, and even a small village like Roy, New Mexico, had a short-lived paper called *El Hispano Americano*.

California had one of the most vocal newspapers, edited by a young *californio* barely twenty years of age who gave his editorials an emphasis seldom seen in other parts of the Southwest. Francisco P. Ramírez was, according to Professor Leonard Pitt, a self-styled champion of the Spanish Americans in California from 1855 to 1859. He named his newspaper *El Clamor Público*, "The Public Outcry," and when he felt that the *californios* were being "sacrificed on the gibbet and launched into eternity" he echoed his sentiments on the editorial page. The *californios* had not been separated from the sources of Spanish as long as the New Mexicans, so they were more familiar with a fuller and more current use of the language. There were other newspapers in California published in Spanish for the benefit of those citizens more accustomed to their original language than to the newly-arrived English language. In San Francisco they read *El Eco del Pacífico* and *La Crónica* until 1856, when these papers also disappeared. It is interesting to note the variety of readers of *El Clamor Público* in Southern California. Ramirez complained that his paper was read more by the Yankees than by the *californios*.

The sum total of newspapers published in Spanish was undoubtedly a factor in keeping the Spanish language alive and functional in the Southwest. There are many Hispanos and Mexican Americans today who are not able to read English, but many of them are able to read Spanish and continue reading it in the local newspapers. Reading, like many skills in the Spanish Southwest, was transmitted by tradition, that is, a father who could read would teach his son enough to get him started, and if he was lucky the child would receive instruction from an itinerant school teacher or at a church school, and would learn not only reading but writing and arithmetic. The number of well-written letters and official records found in the villages and towns throughout the Southwest attest to a greater literacy than is usually recognized. Books were few in the province of New Mexico in colonial days and not particularly abundant in American territorial days; but newspapers provided reading material for those who could read. Occasionally there are interesting old editions of books found in the possession of Hispanic families. Eighteenth century editions of Calderón de la Barca's plays and several volumes bound in vellum, dealing with agriculture, published in Spain in the seventeen hundreds have been found. The mountaineers who owned them complained the books were filled with spelling errors, not knowing the changes that have taken place in Spanish orthography in the past three centuries. A study in 1942, by Eleanor Adams and Dr. France V. Scholes of the University of New Mexico, regarding books in the state between 1598 and 1680, discovered that outside of the missionaries and the Spanish governors of the province, the settlers were credited with only eleven titles, all but one of religious publications.[2] It is quite likely that a close examination of old chests owned by many Hispanos would bring to light some interesting additions.

The most important factor in the preservation of the Spanish language is the rich body of traditional lore which abounds throughout the Southwest in the form of folksongs, proverbs, riddles, games, and folk plays. And even more important are the troubadours and village poets who for centuries have composed songs and ballads in every village of the region, and who in addition to their own compositions have recorded traditional songs and verse of the past. The language of these minstrels of tradition is surprisingly broad and rich in content. They express themselves better than most people in the villages. In trying to put across a message in rhyme they study and use forms of expression that the average individual seldom used. Many present-day urbanized Spanish speakers find it difficult to express themselves in standard Spanish and revert to Anglicized expressions that are neither Spanish nor English but a bastardized form of communication. Many today advocate that these atrocities currently used as Spanish be taught and cultivated because they feel this is the language of the people. The real Spanish speaking folk whom they are trying to emulate have always had a very respectable command of Spanish. The deteriorated forms of expression one hears today are for the most part arbitrary neologisms or Anglicized forms.

The Spanish language has had a different development in each of the principal regions that comprise the Southwest: New Mexico, California, and the Texas-Mexican border. New Mexico was the first province to be settled and was therefore the most isolated from the beginning. The region north of Albuquerque, which was where most of the original colonials settled, was far from the cultural centers of New Spain, as well as from those of Mexico after independence. The only contact the New Mexicans had with people to the south was during the annual Chihuahua fairs and through trading caravans over *El Camino Real* known today as Interstate 25. This isolation, covering two and one half centuries, gave the language of this northern region a distinctive character different from that of the other two regions. Language learning, like other skills in the country, depended to a large extent on oral transmission with the resultant dislocations and mutations to be expected in an isolated region. In addition to the obsolescent words of seventeenth century vintage, there developed in northern New Mexico an intonation not found elsewhere and a pronunciation which is readily recognizable as a distinguishing characteristic of the northern New Mexican colonial. There are in current usage a number of expressions and words which have fallen into disuse in most sectors of the urban Hispanic world. These outmoded forms provide the linguist with interesting cases for study, but they also curtail the use of more current Spanish. The use of such historical forms as *vide, truje, ansí, mesmo, dende, agora,* and a host of other archaic words does not mean that the New Mexicans are speaking incorrect Spanish. It was the language used in the Spanish world when the province was settled at the end of the sixteenth century. It simply means that part of the language these people speak is outmoded.

The relaxed pronunciation in northern New Mexico tends to pass over some of the sounds from off-glide to on-glide without the tension necessary to give phonemes their full value. As a result there are a number of intervocalic and final consonants which are dropped or elided, and "f"s and "s"s are turned into "j"s. *Fuiste* becomes *juites* and *casa* is pronounced *caja*.

The introduction of the English language in the Southwest affected spoken Spanish in all regions in much the same manner but with different degrees of intensity. In the northern villages of New Mexico, no immediate changes became apparent at first because the few Anglo-Americans who settled in this region learned Spanish and used their own language principally for official purposes. The central part of the state, where industry and trade centers were established with the coming of the railroad, had a larger influx of Anglo-Americans. The language lines were soon divided when the modern cities like Albuquerque and Las Vegas grew up near the railroad and the original settlement remained apart and separate about a half mile away, known soon after as "Old Town." This division was characteristic of many cities and towns in the Southwest and reflected the dichotomy of the two languages. English was the language used in business transactions on a larger scale, the official language of administrative and legal matters and the language used exclusively in industry. The Spanish language gradually became the language of the hearth, used in familial situations that did not include the cultural growth of the community. Exposure to English forms of expression, however, expanded the language communication of the Hispanos, who found it more effective to translate literally the new concepts from English into Spanish that was structured on English syntax. This gave rise to such forms as *hacer su mente pa' arriba*, for "to make up your mind." *Tener buen tiempo* was used for "having a good time," *démelo pa' atrás* for "give it back to me," etc. These expressions, so widely used in northern and central New Mexico especially, are hardly conducive to true bilingualism and much less to the claim that the language of Cervantes is being spoken.

The influence of English on the Spanish of the borderlands was inevitable after 1848 because all official and business transactions were carried on in the national language. But it was a mutual influence in many cases. The taking over of the cattle industry included the language of the *vaquero* from the very beginning. Such words as lariat, lasso, horse wrangler, remuda, hackamore, corral, mustang and buckaroo were not far removed from the original Spanish of *la reata, lazo, caballerango, remuda, jáquima, corral, mesteño* and *vaquero*. This phase of western English has been studied for a number of years and continues to be of interest. Dr. Harold W. Bentley made a significant collection about forty years ago of what he called "Spanish terms in English with particular attention to the Spanish Southwest."[3]

The constant traffic of Mexicans and Americans of Mexican descent along the border has served to keep the Spanish language, including regional Mexicanisms, current and alive in this part of the Southwest as already stated. The full meaning of expression available in Spanish from neighboring Mexico has also helped to maintain a fluency in the language which in the isolated north was difficult to attain. Full communication developed along the borderlands with a minimum of Hispanicized English until recently. There are great numbers of the population who are fluent in both languages and who are truly bilingual because they are bicultural. This is a normal consequence of people who grow up in a natural human laboratory where both cultures can be lived and where, as in this case, both English and Spanish are used socially. In the border cities, there are Anglo-Americans who know the Spanish language better than many Mexicans and conversely, there are also Hispanos and Americans of Mexican descent who have a better command of English, both written and spoken, than a large number of Anglo-Americans. There are actually three groups among the Hispanos of the borderlands from California to southern Texas: those who have cultivated English and are more at home in this language, those who prefer Spanish and know it well, along with a working knowledge of English, and the more fortunate ones who have become bilingual for practical reasons. Many professionals of both cultures have found it greatly advantageous to be bilingual. Some of the universities in this borderland have helped to further the cross-cultural flow by undertaking programs in depth through their Centers of Latin American Studies. The Mexican universities too became aware of this interest half a century ago and began offering summer courses for Anglo-American students. From these early efforts the field has grown to such proportions that Mexican universities along the bordering states, as well as the better known ones in the interior, have developed extended programs by adding bicultural Anglo-Americans to their faculties, and many American universities, wishing to take advantage of the cultural climate of a Spanish speaking country, hold summer sessions of their own throughout the neighboring republic. The last step of this mutual program has resulted in an American university in Puebla called the University of the Americas and an extension of the National University of Mexico in San Antonio. Texans say that the southernmost city of their state is Monterrey, and Mexicans insist that their northernmost city is San Antonio.

In California many of the original families, particularly of the more prominent rancheros, assimilated through intermarriage with the incoming Anglo-American traders and sea captains who retired on the west coast. The larger part of their descendants eventually became English speakers. The Spanish-Mexican period in California was comparatively short compared with the settlement of New Mexico which took place at the end of the sixteenth century almost two centuries earlier. Linguistically, this is why there are no archaisms in the language of the *californios* and the later Californians, except those brought in by individuals coming from regions where these language forms developed from an earlier vintage of Spanish. The close relations between the original settlers and the Anglo-Americans in the southern part of the state gave rise to language mixtures which Mexicans have always referred to as *pochismos*. In the years that followed the American occupation, the nickname *pocho* was applied to any person who used an Anglicized version of Spanish, or expressions that were not strictly of Spanish provenience. Some mildly critical quatrains, tempered with Spanish wit, sang the failings of the Californian *pochos* and chided them for their deculturation.

| *Los pochos de California* | The pochos of California |
| *No saben comer tortilla* | Can't even eat tortillas |
| *Porque solo en la mesa* | For at mealtime on the table |
| *Sirven pan con mantequilla* | All they serve is bread and butter |

The influx of Mexicans into the state over the past fifty years has created barrios where the Spanish language is almost exclusively used. But as the children enroll in the public schools where English is taught, Anglicization begins to take place. Unlike the Texas-Mexican border, California does not have good-sized cities adjoining each other along the border where people can freely come and go; as a consequence the carry-over that occurs in cities like El Paso or Laredo does not exist. Both San Diego and Los Angeles require a definite trip of many miles in order to reach the Mexican border. The language situation is comparable to the one in Texas, nevertheless, but with a proportionately smaller number of individuals who speak Spanish exclusively. For one thing, the opportunities to work and mix socially in California are considerably better than they are in Texas, and the cultural climate is more conducive to acculturation. In Texas, with the exception of El Paso and to some extent Laredo, the cultural lines are more strictly drawn.

The one region of the Southwest which probably developed the most complete and colorful Spanish was El Paso Valley, extending north to the village of Doña Ana in southern New Mexico. Being at the crossroads of trade routes, it was never sufficiently isolated to preserve exclusive linguistic forms that eventually would become archaisms. It did preserve, however, a very rich agricultural vocabulary that was not totally current in other parts of the Southwest. Some of this vocabulary was composed of old expressions which disappeared only when modern methods of agriculture were introduced. A study of the Spanish language used up to the early thirties reflects the life that these people led in the country. The urban Hispano with constant contact with Mexico across the border spoke for the most part the language of northern Mexico. Naturally, as the Spanish-speaking population learned English in school and worked in industries established by Anglo-Americans, they found it easier to Hispanize some of the concepts that did not come readily in Spanish, but hardly to the same extent that they did so in the north. The diversified agriculture of the valley, ranging from fruits, vineyards, cereals, cotton, and vegetables in addition to cattle, sheep, hogs, and horse-breeding needed a functional language for such broad and varied activities.

Since agriculture could only be carried on through irrigation, the first residents of the valley had to build a network of ditches based on the guidelines given by the Spanish crown whenever land was parcelled out to settlers. There was the *acequia madre* or mother ditch that took water from the river and distributed it throughout the valley farmlands by a network of smaller *contra acequias*. This called for a number of activities, and also necessitated a person to administer the distribution of water. The man in charge of this was called *alcalde* in the south and *mayordomo* in the north, later replaced by the less picturesque name of "ditch boss." In Arizona this official was known as *zanjero*. In El Paso Valley, the *Alcalde de Agua* title for the supervisor of an *acequia* was used as a carry-over from Spanish colonial days, as was the name *mayordomo* in the north. The Anglo-Americans also perpetuated this title by using the English equivalent of "majordomo" which was close enough to the Spanish word from which it originated. But in the case of *acequia* they followed the southern mountaineer's tendency to use the duo-nominal combination of *"acequia-*ditch" or *"cequia-*ditch" much as the mountaineers would say "man-child" and "rifle-gun."

The preparation of the land for planting required a varied vocabulary in El Paso Valley, where winter plowing was called *barbecho*. In the spring the land was molded into *melgas* or *tablas* for planting alfalfa and wheat, *surcos* and *camellones* for chile and sweet potatoes. The plow opened a *besana* in order to raise *bordos* to hold the water. After planting, they cultivated the plants by hoeing or *escarda*, and if the soil had to be dug deeper, it was called *traspalar*, for which they used an *azadón* rather than the lighter *cavador* used for surface hoeing. In the fall, farmers who had been working on *la labor*, which originally meant 177 acres of farmland, gathered the hay and stacked it in an *harcina* for the winter, or if there was a shed, the hay was placed in a *tejaván*. Perishables such as fruits and vegetables which the families wanted to keep for the winter were placed in an *almárcigo*[4] dug partly into the ground.

Those who had vineyards of Spanish *moscatel* cured some of the grapes into *pasas* which travellers like Gregg and others praised so highly and which California has continued to prepare as a specialty for sale in delicatessens. With the juice of the grape, after making wine, they made a sort of jam called *arrope* to be eaten with *queso añejo*, the aged cheese of the valley. *Asaderos*, an instant type of cooked cheese in the shape of *tortillas* was a favorite for preparing *chile con queso*, a dish which has become well known today and, incidentally, was served at the inauguration of the late President Johnson in Washington not too long ago. From the whey or *suero* that was left after making cheese, the *rancheros* made a sort of cottage cheese called *requesón*, a dish that in Spain is considered a delicacy. They never used the first milk of a cow-come-fresh because they believed that the *calostros* were not fit for human consumption, but after the calf had "brought down the milk," the strippings, called *leche de apoyo*, was considered the richest.

When the colonials in the Valley raised hogs, called *puercos*, but *marranos* or *cochinos* in the north, they confined them in *chiqueros* or *trochiles* unless the farmers were the kind that did things *al trochemoche*, carelessly, and let them fend for themselves. In the fall when the pigs were slaughtered, instead of making ham or bacon like their Anglo-American counterparts from Virginia and Missouri, they preserved the ribs for future use in a sauce called *adobo* and the rest was turned into *salchichas*, *chorizo* and *morcilla* as they do in Mexico and Spain today. From the fat *lonjas* they rendered lard and made the usual *chicharrones*, or *chicharrones de vieja* when made from the rind, the same crackling that is sold today in plastic bags at supermarkets and automobile-filling stations.

This industrious valley where so much history has been made had occasion to use more of the Spanish language of colonial days because of its diversified industry, cattle raising, and constant trade converging from all directions. In trading and selling they needed to measure their products or weigh them when they were sold by weight. So the *almud*, that ancient measure for dry cereals and grains used in northern Spain, was regularly employed until the turn of the century. Some of these quaint measuring boxes varying from one half to a full gallon, were still around in some of the old *ranchos* of the Valley during the early days of the current century. For larger quantities there was the *arroba*, four of which made a *quintal*, or approximately a hundred weight, and a *fanega* which amounted to a bushel and a half.[5] Length and height had a non-verbal system consisting of a number of signs made with hand and arm. It was considered an insult to refer to the height of a boy, for example, by stretching the arm palm down to indicate how tall he was. The insulted party would say, "He's not a horse or a cow." The proper way to indicate the height of a boy was to hold up index finger and thumb outstretched with the index pointing up. An outstretched arm with hand palm down was used for an animal higher than a man's waist and the same arm with hand held vertically, to indicate the height of an animal no higher than the waist, such as a dog or a pig.

Before standards of measurement were established, the folk used the traditionally accepted system understood by all, and served well enough considering that there was no particular need for the precision of modern technology. Since they could not carry around measuring instruments, they used parts of the body to indicate length. The shortest measurement was the inch, indicated by the first joint of the thumb, *pulgada*, derived from the name for thumb, *pulgar*. The next length was *jeme*, the distance between index finger and thumb outstretched, and like the old English equivalent, the Spanish colonials also used the span called *cuarta* or *palmo*. The unopened hand and the individual fingers were occasionally used in measuring liquids in a receptacle as in

English. The next measurement was a *codo*, the distance between the tip of the middle finger and the elbow, and lastly the *vara*, measuring from the center of the chest to the tip of the fingers. There are other traditional ways of measuring length as in the case of mothers who went to market to buy a pair of trousers for a boy. They would ask him to hold the trouser legs outstretched across his chest, assuming that the length across the chest and arms was equivalent to the length of his legs. The same device was used in measuring the length of the saddle stirrup; by holding the stirrup under the armpit and touching the saddle with the finger tips, as any horseman knows today. In measuring land grants, they were not so exact; they calculated distances by so many cigarettes or a day's journey from sun-up to sundown, but when an official grant was made it was expressed in *sitios*, *labores* and *haciendas*, the latter consisting of five *sitios* or five square leagues.

Other interesting archaisms known around El Paso Valley, and not current usually in the northern part of New Mexico, were words referring to everyday living. When speaking about a contemporary of the same age, a person in the Valley would say: "You and I are from the same *camada*," a term that originally meant from the same litter. They wore cotton shirts called *cotones* in the summertime for practical reasons; they were cool, had no buttons and fitted loosely like a slip-over sweater. The name derives from the *cota de malla* or coat of mail used by soldiers in colonial days. When these shirts were made of homespun, they were called *cotón de jerga*. In Spain, the name *jubón* was generally adopted for this shirt, but in the Southwest the older name was preserved. Many old Spanish words had their origin in colonial military dress; *capacete*, is a good example. Originally it was the Spanish helmet worn by the army comparable to the morion. In the Southwest, and particularly in El Paso Valley, it was a covering, not for the head, but a shade for the front seat of a wagon or a buggy. Covered wagons were called *carros encamisados*, that is, wagons with a shirt. In addition to the old words, current since colonial days, the El Paso region also adopted linguistic forms with which they came in contact over *El Camino Real*. This contact with language currently in use has continued to the present day, giving the people of this region along the Mexican border a much broader and up-to-date Spanish vocabulary than those who led a simpler and relatively isolated life in the north.

It is interesting to note that this same region gave rise to the much misunderstood urban argot called *pachuco*, a sort of dialectical Spanish derived arbitrarily from a combination of old Spanish words, Anglicisms, and specially created neologisms understood at the time of their inception by young people, particularly newsboys, Western Union delivery boys, and those who worked at ice cream parlors and candy stores which had bicycle deliveries. At first, it was understood and used extensively in El Paso and nowhere else, but eventually it spread further north and particularly to California. Many original expressions of El Paso argot have become obsolete and have been replaced by a more modern dialect called *pachuco* today. If someone wished to call attention to a good looking girl going by, the girl-watcher would say to his buddy, "*Échale agua, mano!*" which literally meant, "Throw water on her brother!" If attention was being called to something before it passed out of the field of vision, the call was "Lícalo, lícalo!" Going out on the town, so to speak, was expressed by "dar verde," a different color for "painting the town red." If a baseball player pulled a grandstand play by catching a fly ball with one hand, he was said to be giving *changüí*. When a boy was looking for work, he wanted *jale*, but if the work was heavy it was called *camello*. When an El Paso young man was hungry he used to say he had *jaspia*, a condition he easily remedied by going home to his *chante* to *martillar* with his father to whom he respectfully referred to as *jefe*. After dinner, consisting of *maromeros*, the tasty pinto bean, he was ready to *caldear* with his *huisa*, and the girl he made love to did not object to being called by this strange appellation, but if she did, she would tell him, "*Pinte!*" and that meant to "take off." These and scores of other similar expressions current before World War I were so unfamiliar to people in other parts of the Hispanic world that El Pasoans who were members of the clan delighted in speaking their amusing argot in the presence of outsiders in order to confuse and impress them. While this *jerga callejera* was originally contrived as a dialect for the street "Four hundred," it was eventually spread all over the Southwest from California to Colorado and southern Texas where it expanded with numerous borrowings of English slang associated very often with questionable elements of Hispanic society. The region where this argot did not gain much acceptance was the northern mountain villages of New Mexico, where culture was more pastoral than urban.

Cultured individuals found the slang amusing and used a few expressions now and then when speaking to close friends. A medical doctor showing his new car to a friend would say in jest: *"Échele agua a mi nueva catalanga,"* "Throw water on my new chariot." To which the other interlocutor, if he was "hip," would answer in like currency by saying: *"Tres piedras, cuate, y un ladrillo adrenical!,"* meaning that he approved highly, although he actually said: "Three rocks, my twin, and a brick to boot!" Later, this street jargon called *pachuco* assumed social implications and for a while was associated with the dubious elements of Hispanic society in the Southwest. In many sectors of Texas and California it was considered for some time the language of the marijuana smokers, the *grifos*, or *los del tres*, so called because they inhaled the smoke in three gulps. The name *pachuco* is applied both to the speakers and to the dialect because the two go hand-in-hand, but it should not be assumed that those who are familiar with this dialect are also members of the group designated by this term. Like any artificial form of expression, this widely publicized speech lacks originality and has lost much of its former picturesqueness. It ascribes arbitrary meanings to words already known in Spanish lexicon; sometimes it stumbles upon archaic words unknowingly as in the case of *calcos*, from the Latin *calceus*, for shoes, but when it refers to the same article as *boris*, one has an arbitrary invention which is made respectable by calling it a neologism. There is no attempt made to use figurative words or expressions that manifest a sense of beauty; on the contrary, *pachuco* is somewhat depreciatory and inelegant. Oftentimes the Los Angeles zoot-suiters of World War II have been compared with *pachucos*. The former attain their designation from their manner of dress and style of duck-tail haircut. The *pachucos* originated as a linguistic group and have no distinctive dress style.

Folk speech, such as is heard among the mountaineers of New Mexico and the country folk in Mexico is based on observation of nature expressed in colorful figures of speech. For example, people who handle stock have learned that the way to hold a horse with a rope is by leaning sideways on the hip, so they say figuratively, *"Échele cuadril!"* which English-speaking folk working with wagons would render by "Put your shoulder to the wheel." The same Hispanic cowhand speaks of "being thrown over the head" when let down by someone, and expresses it by saying, *"Me echó por la cabeza."* The *pachuco* dialect, on the other hand, being a product of an urban environment, revives a few obsolescent words, makes up a number of Anglicisms and ascribes arbitrary meanings to current Spanish words. Students who have researched the *pachuco* argot have assumed that all the vocabulary used is original, but a simple reference to the dictionary of the Spanish Academy or to a good Spanish-English one will reveal that such words as *chavalo, hacer ronda, garras, greñas, controlar, chaveta* and a number of others listed as *pachuco* are standard Spanish words.

There are attempts being made today to reinstate throughout the Southwest the Spanish language among Americans of Mexican descent, Hispanos of New Mexico, and members of the Chicano movement. One of the problems faced by advocates of what is termed "bilingualism" is the selection of the Spanish that should be taught. Some object to the literary Spanish that forms the standard of Mexico, Latin America, and Spain on the grounds that it is the academic language of the Spanish recognized by the English establishment. Others go so far as to insist that the language be taught as "people speak it." The only problem is the selection of the people to use as the standard for linguistic expression. If the object is to preserve the Spanish language as an instrument of communication among the Mexican-Americans, Hispanos, and Chicanos, the use of a dialect plagued with Anglicisms and syntactical forms derived from the English language would be counter-productive because it is partly molded on the very language they are trying to avoid.

Some Chicano activists advocate the use of what they call "Chicano Spanish" and insist that this is the language that should be taught to them in the public schools because it has more relevance to their culture. This would be a practical consideration if the Chicano adherents did not have to communicate outside the area they live in and if in reality they had a culture of their own. In the Hispanic world, the deteriorated dialect they propose is not acceptable; and since they are not self-sufficient, they must use a language that is understandable and acceptable to both the Spanish speaking and English speaking world. Moreover, the number of Spanish speakers who accept the name Chicano as the label by which they should be identified is indeed small. A recent survey made by the University of Texas Center for Communication Research revealed that 43 percent of the persons interviewed in Texas, Arizona, and California during research for *Teletemas*, a national program to create cultural and entertainment television programming for Mexican-Americans, preferred the term *mexicanos*, while only six percent chose Chicanos. This indicates that the mexicanos who speak the Spanish spoken throughout the Hispanic world prefer to stay within the culture that gave birth to the Spanish language. Mexico has produced a literature that is recognized throughout the world, and the present advances in all fields of Mexican economy, industry, and education have found their language adequate for world communication. The Chicanos, who are an infinitesimal number in the Hispanic world, would isolate themselves completely if they adopted the dialect they choose in their attempts to create a Chicano literature. The Spanish language of the Southwest has a very long history, a history that dates back to Mexico and Spain. A fluent command of Spanish today is what Hispanic students in the Southwest are striving for and not a dialectical expression made up of Anglicisms and perverted Spanish idiom. This is probably the reason why an overwhelming majority prefer the term *mexicano*, with a sprinkling of "Mexican American," "Latin American," and even "Tejano."

The Southwest will ideally continue to use Spanish and English for cultural and historical reasons. The problem arises when we try to keep both at an equal level of usage. Bilingualism, however, is another long story.

Those who insist that the few archaisms of sixteenth century vintage be preserved do not take into account what all students of history and language know, namely, that a language is a mirror of civilization and culture. A verb-form that became obsolescent a hundred years ago does not reflect the society of a modern Spanish speaker.

There is a third group of Spanish language advocates who use English and Spanish simultaneously on the assumption that this is the way the language is actually spoken today. It is not bilingualism, strictly speaking, because neither of the two languages appears in its entirety. It is a sort of mixture used particularly for writing verse. Four-letter words in English appear with their Spanish counterparts as part of the freedom of expression which versifiers feel should be used bilingually. The resulting effect from this combination is not a happy one because of the different manner in which scatological language is used in Spanish. There is a hoary tradition in this form of composition found in the unbowdlerized versions of the Middle Ages, especially among the poets of the literary court of Don Juan II. This tradition has continued unbroken throughout Latin America. *Picardía Mexicana* published by the Mexican contemporary scholar A. Jiménez is a collection of all types of scatological verse designed to be witty and entertaining but with no thought of being poetic.[6] The picaresque language of Spain was also cultivated by the *léperos* and the *pelados* of Mexico, who may be considered the forerunners of the modern *pachucos*. Even the traditional bards of the Southwest use the *picardía* very effectively in some compositions written in a lighter vein.

In the midst of these considerations, the federal government has been asked to underwrite a program of bilingual education for the Southwest as a means of preserving the linguistic heritage of the Spanish speakers. Advocates of bilingualism have not yet reached a consensus regarding the type of Spanish which should be cultivated. It will be interesting to learn what criteria will eventually be adopted to determine the nature of the Spanish language which is to be taught if and when bilingual education becomes an accepted program. In some cases, recommendations have already been implemented by active advocates of bilingualism who are preparing materials for classroom use. The San Diego Public Schools publish a magazine called *Materiales en Marcha* under a Title VII grant which has attained wide distribution within a few months.[7] The content of the publication is bilingual, although the Spanish contributions are too few, and the material is biculturally oriented with the expressed purpose of being "both educational and entertaining." The Spanish used by contributors is that of educated native speakers with no attempt made to use the dialectal speech advocated by other groups. The same is true of *Bilingual Educational Services* published in South Pasadena.[8] This is a catalogue of films, film strips, and a variety of audio-visual aids taken directly from Spanish-speaking countries and consequently prepared in the current Spanish used universally. In an extensive workshop conducted at San Jose State for the preparation of materials recommended for bilingual education, the director, Dr. Feliciano Rivera, obtained a good deal of material from the Ministry of Education in Mexico City. Again, the language was the current speech of the Mexican republic. In Berkeley there is a quarterly with an entirely different orientation in regard to language and content. *El Grito*, as this quarterly is called, is a contentious publication which includes articles written in English or in Spanish, except that there is no fixed standard for the language used by the authors. All brands of language appear, from the literary lexicon to Pachuco and Chicano dialect. For example, "Nuestra Circunstancia Lingüística" by Rosaura Sánchez is not only a good study of southwestern Spanish phonology and morphology but also a good example of contemporary, academic style.[9] The policy of the magazine is quite liberal, and since it is not intended as pedagogical material for use in the classroom, contributing authors are allowed to use their own choice of Spanish. The wide variety of efforts to further the use of the Spanish language in public education will eventually determine the choice of Spanish which will be taught when a formal program is implemented. The interest manifested in the preservation of the original language of the southwesterners, whether Hispanos, Mexican Americans, or members of the Chicano movement, should produce something interesting and valuable. It is too early yet to appraise the results of these efforts, but in another decade or two there should be results of measurable magnitude, providing that the choice of what to teach and speak is allowed to develop freely and unhindered by contentious political considerations. Hopefully, this concern and renewed interest in the Spanish language and culture should eventuate in its restitution to a practical and effective level throughout the Southwest.

## NOTES

1. Aurelio M. Espinosa, *Studies in New Mexican Spanish*, in Bulletin University of New Mexico, 1, 2 Language Series, 1909.
2. Eleanor Adams and France V. Scholes, "Books in New Mexico," (Reprint) in *New Mexico Historical Review*, 1942, p. 44.
3. Harold W. Bentley, *A Dictionary of Spanish Terms in English*, (New York: Columbia University Press, 1932).
4. The words *harcina, tejaván,* and *almarcigo* are characteristic of the changes made by the folk in the Southwest. The current Spanish is *hacina, almácigo* and *tejavana*. The first two words have added the trilled *r*, a reinforcement known as epenthesis, and *tejaván* is shortened by the relaxed pronunciation of the final *a* which eventually disappeared.
5. When the merchants weighed the produce of El Paso Valley they used *romanas, básculas, pesas* or *balanzas*. The medieval *romana*, probably of Roman origin as the name indicates, was replaced by a newer model consisting of an encased spring with a vertical dial and a hook that held the article being

weighed. When a container, carrier or receptacle was used in weighing they adjusted the scale for the *tara* or "tare." The adjustment was called *destarar*.

6. A. Jiménez, *Picardía Mexicana*, (México, D.F.: 1960), Libro Mex Editores.

7. "Materiales en Marcha," ESEA Title VII, San Diego City Schools, 2950 National Avenue, San Diego, California, 92113.

8. *Bilingual Educational Materials*, 1508 Oxley St., South Pasadena, California, 91030.

9. Rosa Sánchez, "Nuestra Circunstancia Lingüística," *El Grito*, 6, 1, Fall 1972, pp. 45-72.

# On Chicano History: In Memoriam, George I. Sánchez 1906-1972

**JESUS CHAVARRIA**

> we do
> our shadows live
>
> *Alurista*

Given the nature of this encuentro, it may be that many of my co-contributors responded somewhat as I did when I first received Américo Paredes' invitation to contribute to a volume dedicated to the memory of George I. Sánchez. It did not take long for me to reply an acceptance. And I further suspect that many of us might have done the same pretty much for the same reasons. Although not having known him well personally—we were of different generations and only met twice—I knew of him since the mid-fifties and followed his work over the years. Entre nosotros in education, most everyone had heard of him and respected him and his work, and so for those of us joined in this volume it is, I am sure, a distinct honor to write some words in his memory.

    As I recall, one of Sánchez's most important achievements—and this should especially be taken to heart by Chicano youth—was his protest, begun as early as 1934, against so-called IQ tests and the placement of Chicano children in public school tracking systems. Very early in his professional life, Sánchez began his battle against the public schools for spoiling the learning capacities of our youth. At the age of twenty-eight he already recognized the impact of such losses on our human, cultural, and social status in this country. Over the years, as we all know, he continued his protest, and he always impressed us with his quiet confidence and infectious optimism.

I last saw him in July of 1971. We met on a quiet and sunny summer day on the University of Texas campus in Austin in his office, and despite his illness, the vigor of his confidence in our chances as people remained as strong and radiant as the sun outside. We spoke a bit about the new Chicano politics and about the movement of the youth; his words and gestures made it clear that his spirit still marched right alongside them in their protest. It also became clear, in an understated kind of way, that he was fully aware of some differences. From what I knew of him, and due to that brief encounter which remains a unique experience in my memories of the late sixties and early seventies, it is perhaps not inaccurate or unfair to say that his life's work, and perhaps even his hopes, are being fulfilled in the efforts and hopes of the human struggle which some of us know as the Chicano Movement.

We also share with him and with his generation a common history and culture (which ultimately represent the genetic pool of politics). We know of course that on more than one occasion he referred to our history as the history of a "forgotten people"—that was then the cry to make in the wilderness. However, we of the generation of el sesenta, because of our different generational experience in this country, have chosen to call it instead Chicano history. Our respective views on history notwithstanding, it still seems to me that these propositions on the value and meaning of Chicano history are in harmony with our remembrance of Sánchez's life and work.

I

It is well to remember that the Chicano history which is increasingly talked about today in educational institutions and political circles first appeared as a category of history in the colleges and universities of California in the mid-sixties. Those of us who then used the term might not have had a clear idea of just what we meant by it, but we did know what it did not mean. It did not mean to us (and our resistance to this part of our past was unquestionable) that so-called history which begins with a few chapters "about México," and then concludes with a few chapters about Mexican Americans in San Antonio and Los Angeles and raps about discrimination and police brutality. Neither did we mean those histories that invoke populist rhetoric about Pancho

Villa and Zapata, or those that picture us as wayward sons and daughters of Mexican culture and history. For as we all know, nosotros no somos, como dice la canción, "mexicanos de acá de este lado." That is not the kind of history we had in mind, though at the time about the only thing we could say on Chicano history was that what we had in mind was knowledge of that unique and distinctive concrete social process that had shaped us as a people and which had occurred at a certain time and in a certain place. Our earliest discussions on Chicano history—which took place among Chicano youth and which were truly extraordinary in range and depth—happened during the very active years of the Chicano Movement of the late 1960s.

We talked of la cuestión Chicana endlessly it seems, and continually thought of it and in time started to dream about it, sometimes as haunting nightmares that confused us terribly. We also discussed it at conferences, meetings, and caucuses; one weekend at Davis, another at Riverside, next at Los Angeles, then on to San Diego, Fresno, San Bernardino, etcetera, on through the years. Every day in the years that followed, we lived through a thousand crises in our practice of a Chicano consciousness, and after every crisis we asked ourselves in intense frustration, "Why do these things keep happening to us? To me?" But we kept on moving, going forward. That is how we started becoming aware of our contradictions, at the personal and at the social level, and how we began to look toward Chicano history as a source of knowledge about our existential situation.

If we look back, those of us who lived those moments (and there were many of us), it seems rather clear that the main energy behind the idea of Chicano history came from a deeply felt need by our people for self-knowledge, for personal and social knowledge about our social and sexual past in this country since at least the middle of the nineteenth century. In the process of piercing that initially veiled and dreamy encounter with our past, we arrived at the category of "Chicano" as culturally, historically, and psychologically illuminating. *Chicanismo* simply came to mean asserting our very own distinctive and unique natures and characters as a people. Así fue como descubrimos que no éramos simplemente pochos and certainly we were not "Americans" in any sense of the word that would have civil and economic validity. It seems quite clear that there existed a relationship between a socially expressed need to know oneself—which was the heart of the Chicano Movement—and the creative explosion of hundreds of literary works and newspapers; of the flowering of a militant poetry ringing with assertive cantos as in Corky's *Joaquín* and the soul-searing versos of Alurista; of the renaissance in mural arts in San Antonio, Fresno, and Oakland; of the farmworkers' and Valdez's teatro campesino; and of a social movement which produced a program of higher education called Chicano Studies and also Chicano history.

The novel spirit of Aztlán, of the myth of the eternal return, is the energy force that inspired one of the leading statements of the Chicano Movement in California college and university campuses, *El Plan de Santa Bárbara*, a collectively executed plan of action (the result of a conference originally proposed by René Núñez), brought together, among others, by Armando Valdez, Juan Gómez-Quiñones, and Fernando de Necochea. In *El Plan* we find in its first sentence, expressed the spirit of the times in the words: "For all people, as with individuals, the time comes when they must reckon with their history." We can go so far as to say that the Chicano Movement in the colleges and universities of California created the idea of Chicano history, and fragments of the idea or its entirety could be heard wherever and whenever Chicanos gathered on the many campuses and towns of California as far north as Davis in the late 1960s.

It thus seems safe to say that Chicano history emerged as a product of the Chicano Movement because of our people's social and psychic need to gain self-knowledge. There were also other attributes which inspired Chicano history, such as that parallel to our need for self-knowledge. We also gradually recognized that we were the social and cultural product of a racial and cultural mestizaje which had attained such a degree of deranged assimilation that it had produced a monstrous distortion of our true past. Self-consciously we thus set out to identify and reconcile ourselves with our true past, which meant a positive identification with our indigenous forebears.

That is the feeling which eventually engendered the rebirth of the myth of Aztlán, which prefigures the return of a cycle of time out of our past that is slowly emerging from the texture of our memories.

Yet the attributes of the Chicano Movement and of Chicano history did not always appear so arcane, and so we also conceived of ourselves in the rational sense of social class. That is why from the start Chicano history especially focused on workers in the fields or in the urban colonias.[1] That too reflected the reality of the Movement, for its social impetus essentially came from maturing workers and middle classes increasingly conscious of their political rights and, more importantly, of new skills in exercising them. The fact that the farmworkers of California, the lumpen-proletariat of northern New Mexico, or the urban youth of Colorado and California were initially among the most strident voices expressing the new mood of the sixties is implicit and explicit to the writing, so far, of a Chicano history that has stressed problems such as the composition of the Chicano labor force, a variety of strikes in key industries, and the mobilization of several kinds of workers' organizations.

In sum, though there may not be complete agreement on this point, Chicano history shared from the start the fundamental attributes of the Chicano and Chicana Movement itself: a passion for self-awareness, for pursuing our own unique consciousness, and a deeply-felt need to know about the shaping influence of race and class on human society and on individual character and personality as well as on culture.

Looking back over the last few years it seems clear that those were the problems that Chicano history initially set out to explain, and due to our most recent experiences we have begun to understand a few more, but before going any further along these lines we should look at the nature of the past itself.

II

Before passing to the actual datum of Chicano history there are two questions, interrelated and interdependent, that must be taken into account, the first being the question of the relationship between Chicano history and culture and the history and culture of México. What that question actually implies is an even larger one: the vital question whether we are, or are not, a unique and distinctive people in history. Most of us probably agree, or so it would seem, that these two questions figure among the most strategic problems dealing with our particular existential situation as a distinct people.

Ultimately what is the fundamental problem of Chicano history but that of explaining the historical becoming of our distinctive and unique being, or existence. Only through Chicano history can we truly answer the question of whether we are or are not ourselves; or whether we are simply the other (either the other from México, or the other from the United States).

Perhaps such a manner of looking at ourselves will appear to some as an enlightened way for us to start dealing with our vital statistics as citizens of the United States. Who are we? Are we simply mexicanos who speak English and who have forgotten our Mexican ways?

If we truly mean to explore Chicano history, then it seems to me that these are the kinds of questions that we must confront. We are starting out by saying, then, that if we speak of Chicano history it is because we sense enough of its nature as to suggest its distinctiveness; a distinctiveness that derives from the unique experience of our forebears, beginning in the middle of the nineteenth century when we first appear as a unique community due to a fundamental conflict between the expanding capitalism of the United States and the weak neocolonial social structures of a México beset by profound inner contradictions. Since those difficult times the major conditioner of our becoming an increasingly distinctive population has been the relative power relations between México and the United States. All of the fundamental facts of life behind our vital statistics have been affected by that basic relationship.

Seen in this light, obviously, Chicano history is not simply an extension of Mexican history but potentially an autonomous variant. I am not saying simply that we are a unique people in history because of our peculiar historical experiences which have produced a unique culture, but also because perhaps our historical aspirations may be different from those of México. Asserting our distinctiveness should not however be construed as a denial of our origins in the culture and civilization of ancient and modern México, for it means mainly that the historical origins most immediate to us, not only in time but also in space, are those experiences accumulated since the late sixteenth century in the lands variously called el norte, or the Spanish borderlands, or the American southwest, or by some of us, Aztlán. That is our true culture area, for in those lands appeared some of the most important distinctions between Mexican society and culture and what, in time, will become known as Chicano society and culture.

Actually any proper discussion of our hypothesis should start with the sixteenth century. To do so we need but turn to George Sánchez's classic, *Forgotten People,* first published in 1940. "Fruits of Conquest," his first chapter, resounded with the somewhat bothersome noises "of trumpets" and the blinding "glistening of armor," but nevertheless it included a good general description of the founding of New Mexican society. It tells a marvelous story of the origins of the New Mexican as the unfolding of a new mestizo culture, part sixteenth-century Spain and part "pueblo . . . Navajo . . . Mexican Indian." Just as a new blood appeared in Nuevo México, so did a new hybrid culture, both the product of the mixing of blood and culture of the Spaniard and the native of the place (or brought there from México)—in effect a mineral synthesis of race, culture, and environment. According to Sánchez, such early efforts soon produced a "simple agrarian economy," which in turn supported a unique pastoral culture and society characterized by forms of "communalism." Gradually, social stratification also occurred, indeed it came with the original settlers. By and large a healthy patrimonialism reigned, occasionally highlighted by the celebration of "saints' days, marriages, christenings, and baptisms." Most of this happened in the seventeenth and eighteenth centuries in Nuevo México, and in the 1700s a similar society and culture flowered in California and Texas. Some important differences, of course, existed between the society and culture which Sánchez described and, say, California—for example, the independence of México deeply affected the economy of California but left Nuevo México virtually untouched. Nevertheless, on the whole the two societies shared relatively similar social structures, in addition to sharing their common origins in México. Our common origins in México, however, as Sánchez pointed out, were gradually modified by the relative autonomy the regions of the northern periphery enjoyed, and thus a kind of distinctive society evolved imperceptibly but surely.[2] Up to this point what distinguished our people from the people of México was their peculiar, rustic ways of coping with their environment. Jacinto Quirarte, for instance, has recently drawn our attention to the distinctive regional art and architecture of our forebears.[3]

Up to the middle of the nineteenth-century (earlier in the case of Texas), we are dealing clearly with what we may tentatively call the colonial period of our entire social history, and fortunately there exists a formidable research literature on the subject. Our major task in relation to this period is therefore to conceptualize it from a Chicano perspective. Dr. Gómez-Quiñones recently wrote: "The historiography related to Chicano history is richest in dealing with the period of the sixteenth, seventeenth, and eighteenth centuries. Perhaps in this period . . . research is not as imperative as is a re-examination and reinterpretation of the available sources."[4] It is vital that we develop a conceptual approach to this period, and then proceed to investigate the distinctive historical experiences of our people up to the middle of the nineteenth century. What we need are answers to such questions as, What were the peculiar social relations that characterized community life in Aztlán from the sixteenth to the early nineteenth centuries? and What type of culture did such relations produce? This means that we must start by conceptualizing the mode of production of those particular social relations—what were the influencing institutions, such as property and law, and what was the division of labor. We must also determine the nature of the impact of such relations on consciousness and the making of culture—what were the dominating ideologies and what relations existed between female and male. It is important that in approaching this period we give critical attention not only to the conceptual problems but also to the problems of method, ultimately for the research to extend beyond published materials.

Yet for all the importance of the colonial period, the distinctiveness of our culture essentially derives most immediately from the nineteenth century, when starting with the secession of Texas and then with the Mexican War a major derangement took place in the lands of Aztlán.

III

Although the drama of Chicano history as it is understood here truly begins, in violent, modern terms, in the second half of the nineteenth century, at least some of its distinguishing features can already be delineated in the first half of the century. Relations between the native populations of Aztlán and "Americans" from the United States (as well as of other encroaching European populations) were characterized, gradually but inexorably, by the absorption of the former by the latter from early in the century. Fear of the encroaching North Americans was expressed as early as the late eighteenth century by Spanish frontier authorities, and it is certainly significant how intermarriage between the daughters of well-to-do Californio families and Yankee traders and men of adventure starts to take place with all of the rigor of a seemingly calculated policy by at least the 1830s. Other aspects of social relations tend to confirm this trend of events, such as in political terms the separation of Texas in the 1830s, and the economic fact that by the 1840s, due to the trade of the Santa Fe Trail, North Americans already dominated the economy of Nuevo México. During the early part of the century perhaps the greatest weakness of the society and culture of Aztlán, from which stemmed its vulnerability, was its relative isolation and its small, scattered population, which amounted to between 65,000 and 75,000 inhabitants prior to 1848; spread out in a vast rural backland and in towns such as San Antonio, Santa Fe, Tucson, San Diego, and Monterey. As one would expect, a marked localism characterized this society.

Beginning with the events of Texas in the 1830s, but more particularly due to the U.S.–Mexican War of 1846–48, the entire culture area of Aztlán was conquered and assimilated by an expanding United States. From then on the native population became selectively absorbed, according to the needs and demands of the dominant society, from which there evolved a relatively perceptible pattern of social and cultural relations between the native Californios, Hispanos, and Tejanos and the Anglo population.

There already exists some relative agreement among Chicanos that the second half of the nineteenth century is the crucial period for the emergence of the Chicano. Alvarez conceptualizes the period somewhat vaguely with the category of "the creation generation." He writes, "The Mexican American people were created abruptly, virtually overnight, because Mexico suffered military defeat."[5] Moreover, he characterizes relations between Chicanos and Anglos as being conditioned by a "thoroughly structured, thoroughly defined, social situation."[6] What actually happened is that the social process engendered in the aftermath of the war progressively deranged the prewar society and culture of the area. In time this process became the major conditioner of a new society and culture, one principally characterized by a structural dependency. Out of such peculiar social circumstances, a novel kind of bilingualism and biculturalism evolved, as well as a novel social type, the Chicano.

Not all the population fared equally bad under the new social order. Some "upper class families . . . became so thoroughly Americanized as to be able to slip into Anglo-American society at will."[7] In general, however, wholesale class and racial exploitation ensued which despite the efforts of social bandits (such as Tiburcio Vázquez, Joaquín Murieta, Elfego Baca, Juan N. Cortina, Gregorio Cortéz),[8] produced in California the "alienation of the second generation" (between 1865 and 1890).[9] Between the midcentury and 1900, the social history of the area now responded to new demands which created a social situation that has been characterized by Leonard Pitt thusly:

> Of the forty-five Californios representing the twenty-five families whom Thomas Oliver Larkin had enumerated in 1846 as the 'principal men' of the old régime, the vast majority went to their graves embittered. Indeed, the gentry had experienced what might be called California's only true social revolution: they were a ruling class militarily conquered, bereft of national sovereignty and a constitutional framework, and alienated from their land, homes, civil rights, and honor. They had retained little else besides their religion and a thin residue of honorary political influence.[10]

The lower classes of course fared even worse. Between 1854 and 1865, sixteen to twenty percent of San Quentin inmates were Californios or Mexicanos—"a high figure in view of the relative numerical decline of the Spanish-speaking."[11] In the case of Texas, "by 1900 the Mexican's role in Texas as a landless and dependent wage laborer was well established in all but a few insignificant areas."[12] Such were the adverse circumstances, the birth trauma, that marked our emergence as a people.

In view of such events, what can we make of this period on the whole? It means that once again we must turn to the conceptual problem. In so doing we find ourselves a little more advanced than in dealing with the colonial or formative period. While we do not yet fully understand the period from the sixteenth to the eighteenth centuries enough to conceptualize fully its meaning, discussion among us thus far has produced a tentative hypothesis about the nineteenth century. Among Chicanos, the most advanced conceptual proposal made to date for explaining our social status in this country is the viewpoint which refers to our past and present situation as essentially the product of a colonialist experience.[13] Without a doubt the most developed historical particularization of that point of view has been the excellent essay by Rodolfo Acuña, *Occupied America: The Chicano's Struggle Toward Liberation*. Acuña's essay is the first full-length history of Chicanos to adhere to a Chicano chronology—that is, that starts in mid-nineteenth century and then proceeds forward. Early in the essay Acuña writes:

> Central to the thesis of this monograph is my contention that the conquest of the Southwest created a colonial situation in the traditional sense—with the Mexican land and population being controlled by an imperialistic United States. Further, I contend that

this colonization—with variations—is still with us today. Thus I refer to the colony, initially, in the traditional definition of the term, and later (taking into account the variations) as an internal colony.[14]

Acuña then continues in the following pages to characterize the colonial situation on historical and analytical grounds and likens the social experience of Chicanos to that of Third World peoples.[15] While others have also used the concept of "internal colony" in relation to the Chicano people, Acuña's essay is perhaps the most complete and extensive formulation to date.

Nonetheless, and despite the fact that analytically the colonialist thesis does make a lot of sense, it is perhaps not entirely valid historically. It is valid, say, up to the end of the Mexican period of Aztlán, but thereafter its application, and especially the application of the concept of "internal colony," raises some complex problems. It is quite clear, for example, that if at a rather general level of analysis there does exist a parallelism between the social experience of Third World peoples and Chicanos, at a level of particularizing our historical experiences as Chicanos the historical record diverges.

Rather, I propose that we view ourselves as a dependent national minority instead of as an internal colony. My major reservation to the concept of internal colonialism derives from the fact that in order for a colonialist situation to exist there must first exist an articulated and formal system of political control effectuated through an administrative system. While economic motivation may be the major impulse behind colonial aggrandizement, the colonial situation still requires a political rationale (ideology) and a system of control (the colonial administration). Also, for a colonialist situation to exist there must exist a colonial policy. As Chicanos, however, such has not been our lot. It is a point of legal fact that we have never been formally recognized as a conquered people, for the provisions of the Treaty of Guadalupe Hidalgo have never been formally recognized. As far as the federal government of the United States is concerned, and the state and municipal governments as well, we do not exist as a people—for there does not exist either public policy or legislation which establishes such rights. That is why Sánchez referred to us as a *"forgotten people,"* and it is from that source too that stems the notion of our being an *"invisible minority."* For in the eyes of white Anglos we do not exist. We do not have a culture and neither do we have a history—we have no identity. If we were colonized we would at least have a name, but we do not; we are simply "the Spanish-speaking," a phrase which tells virtually nothing about us. Our situation, therefore, is not comparable to the status of the colonized, for a colonialist situation requires a formal recognition of the status of the colonized, and the establishment of a system of administration and public policy to perpetuate it. That has not been our lot because we have never been granted formal recognition.

Thus, it behooves us to establish the basis of our own identity by first establishing the historical basis of our own unique and distinctive culture; and in order for us to do so it is well that we grapple with the problem of conceptualizing the meaning of that experience. To see ourselves as a dependent national minority means that we are able to assimilate at the level of social analysis the experience of colonized people, yet we do not lose sight of the important fact that we have never been granted formal recognition. Moreover the concept of dependent national minority has the added advantage of proposing a nationalist character to the Chicano struggle. As a dependent *national* minority we struggle to vindicate our rights, which are first and foremost to eliminate our dependence on an alien culture and to give our community a just and necessary measure of economic and political independence. On the matter of Chicano nationalism there is obviously a great need for further discussion, especially in relation to the need for formulating a revolutionary Chicano nationalism. All this is not to say that the Chicano Movement should not be a part of the international struggle for the vindication of the oppressed peoples of the world.

At this time the thrust of these remarks is intended mainly to invite comments on the suggestion that it was beginning in the second half of the nineteenth century that we first appeared as a new dependent national minority in the United States. It is in that era that begins our "national period"—or that period from 1848 to 1919—during which we were assimilated, according to an informal system of social relations, as a dependent racial minority. All of our history since 1848 is a reflection of that process, and it is only now, with the appearance of Chicano history, that we are becoming aware of our national existence and status.

Just as we proposed in relation to the colonial period the necessity for a certain kind of historiography, similarly there is a need to do the same for the period 1846–1919. We have already seen how we are more advanced in dealing with the conceptual problem of this period than in dealing with the former; we also have, it seems, a greater knowledge about this period. Or perhaps I should qualify this by saying that we seem to have greater materials about the kinds of institutions which the Anglos established, though not about the impact of those institutions on our society and culture. Indeed, that should become the first item on our research agenda for this period, the study of how Anglo institutions, culture, and language affected our people in the course of the 1800s and early 1900s.

In focusing on this crucial aspect of social relations between Anglos and Chicanos, we should keep in mind especially the concept of dependency. We should first distinguish between psychological dependence, such as that involving mother and child, and social dependence, or that condition which assumes the social dependence of, in our case, a racially and culturally distinct people, on the institutions and culture of a dominant, foreign, institutional and cultural matrix. Unlike the blacks, Asians, and even the Native Americans, we have a unique status of dependence—one whose distinctive feature is a presumed invisibility—and that has produced our distinctive consciousness, our distinctive linguistic and cultural configurations. For example, we still do not know what to call ourselves and lack a formally recognized status, both conditions which redound to our political impotence. So the concept of dependence is also central to any discussion related to the problem of how to conceptually approach the period 1846–1919. For the moment it is perhaps enough to draw attention to these two periods: the two periods which run from 1846 up to 1919, and the much larger one which begins with the sixteenth and culminates in the eighteenth century.

## IV

In the final analysis, what is the meaning and value of Chicano history? Will it, can it, contribute to our freedom in face of the harsh realities of our social circumstance? Surely only individual raza can render such a judgment, and surely too, the struggle to verify and confirm our own perceptions and feelings about the past has only begun. Nevertheless, we can suggest some perhaps useful observations on what the value and meaning of such an idea of Chicano history might be, in time.

First, it is vitally important to realize that such an idea of Chicano history serves a social function, in that it can help illuminate problems in schooling, in anthropology, in social work, in politics, and even deeply personal problems of consciousness. We need only remind ourselves of the axiom that the way we view the past is also the way we view ourselves, in order to grasp the strategic importance of historical knowledge. Until a short time ago, Chicanos were so caught up with the constant and daily struggle of social and psychic living that we hardly had time for such things. Then, in the 1960s, our society experienced a kind of crisis, from which there appeared a need to enlighten ourselves about our past. At that moment, when our people assigned an importance to historical knowledge, we encountered and began a social process governed by historical time. To begin to consider the problem of Chicano culture in terms of history is indeed to achieve, in our social analysis and intuitive adventures, the depth of time.

Long before the 1960s, of course, we had known histories about ourselves—indeed George Sánchez's classic *Forgotten People* is representative of an old tradition—but the Chicano history of the sixties started something new with its thesis of the distinctive evolution of our society and culture. It further proposed that we measure and assess critically our community in terms of a social and cultural process extending over time. At the moment when a community begins to see itself as constituting a chain of events that occur within time, then perhaps one starts to understand a little about why certain things happen—to me, to you, to everyone.

One starts to learn about social institutions, about their structural organization and spiritual natures; one begins to learn about culture and how it comes to be formed and shaped, especially one's material and spiritual experience, and about individual consciousness, and how it is influenced and determined by race, class, sex, and language.

Certainly that is one value that historical knowledge has; that it can approximate and even become an experience of revelation, mainly because of its power to divine the mysteries of culture and also of consciousness. For history, seen as process of becoming, contains the elements of culture just as it also contains the elements of consciousness. Without a historical perspective rooted in the material as well as subjective conditions which have shaped our lives, we could never understand how it was that we came to be—our peculiar cultural situation which involves a unique speech, particular arts, an increasingly peculiar scholarship and politics, in short, a peculiar Chicano style. True, the purists will surely shift restlessly at such bizarre suggestions, and in chorus chant that our culture is characterized mainly by its great and opulent variety, and who can deny it. It is certainly true that our way of life is marked by a rich and rare variety—one need only compare California to Texas—but it is also characterized by a fundamental unity at the level of structure. Despite the great variety of functions, determinations, and particularizations that exist among us, there also exist certain structural uniformities which when we finally start to recognize them will contribute to a greater solidarity of purpose among us. There are infinite variations in that continuum of relations that exist between Anglo society and culture and Chicanos in Texas and California, but, are not such differences determined to a considerable degree by the relative development of the Anglo society and culture of Texas and California—i.e., differences among them have different impacts on Chicanos and hence determine differences among us.

If we suggest that history can be the key to understanding our unique and distinctive culture, it can also be proposed that at the very least it should inform our politics as well. Once more it is the dynamic view of society and culture that history can project which could contribute to a truly enlightened Chicano politics. There is one strategic contribution that Chicano history can make to a Chicano politics, and that is to help us understand the process of changing society, particularly given the reality of certain circumstances. For the most part change among us, given our relative powerlessness, has mainly reflected change in the larger society. By and large we need and want what the larger society needs and wants. Since such needs and wants involve some of the bare necessities of life—such as housing, employment, schooling opportunities—that is clearly understandable. Yet perhaps we also need, and want, to develop a more creative approach to change, so that we can change our lives in order to be closer to our true selves. We are perhaps standing at a juncture where it might be possible to strike towards a new direction. What is it that we want to change? Into what? For what? Should change simply be the end result of what the political marketplace will give? Or perhaps we also need to address an even larger question: Do we really want to change?

In sum, the meaning and value of our history lies in the fact that it can be the key to understanding our culture; that it can enlighten our politics, among other things, on the problem of changing; and that it can even have the function of revealing to us our consciousness.

## V

According to George Sánchez' thesis, we were a "forgotten people" because "in the march of imperialism a people were forgotten, cast aside as the byproduct of territorial aggrandizement." From that near-fatal eventuality derived most of our misfortunes, yet George Sánchez belonged to a generation that saw in education—according to the Mexican and western liberal tradition—an open road toward freedom. Only if we had access to education could we manage and cope with the world, and that became the essence of his message.

We of the generation of el sesenta, share in that point of view with him, though perhaps our concepts of education and knowledge differ from his, which is understandable given the unfolding circumstances of our society and culture. Nonetheless, we can feel a solidarity with him, even now; a solidarity which will surely grow through the years in recognition of the life path which he took and which we must now follow.

## NOTES

1. See *Aztlán* and *El Grito* for numerous articles, such as Ronald W. López, "The El Monte Berry Strike of 1933," *Aztlán* (Spring 1970); and, Salvador Enrique Alvarez, "The Legal and Legislative Struggle of the Farmworkers, 1965-1972," *El Grito* (Winter 1972-73).
2. See Leonard Pitt's *The Decline of the Californios* (Berkeley: University of California Press, 1966), esp. chapter one, and David J. Weber, ed., "Selected Pages from *Foreigners in Their Native Land*," (Albuquerque: University of New Mexico Press, 1973), pg. 4f.
3. Jacinto Quirarte, *Mexican American Artists* (Austin: University of Texas Press, 1973), pg. 30.
4. Juan Gómez-Quiñones, "Toward a Perspective on Chicano History," *Aztlán* (Fall 1971), pg. 11.
5. Rodolfo Alvarez, "The Psycho-Historical Experience of the Mexican American People," *Social Science Quarterly* (June 1971), pg. 20.
6. Ibid., pg. 19.
7. Rodman W. Paul, "The Spanish-Americans in the Southwest, 1848-1900," in John G. Clark, ed., *The Frontier Challenge* (Lawrence, 1971), pg. 34.
8. Pedro Castillo and Albert Camarillo, *Furia y Muerte* (Los Angeles: UCLA Chicano Studies Center, Publications, 1973).

9. Pitt, *Californios*, pg. 262.
10. Ibid., pg. 278.
11. Ibid., pg. 256.
12. Leo Grebler, et al., *The Mexican American People* (New York: The Free Press, 1970), pg. 49.
13. See Mario Barrera, Carlos Muñoz, and Charles Ornelas, "The Barrio as Internal Colony," in Harlan Hahn, ed., *People and Politics in Urban Society: Urban Affairs Annual Review* (Beverly Hills: Sage Publications, 1972); and Tomás Almaguer, "Toward the Study of Chicano Colonialism," *Aztlán* (Spring 1971).
14. Rudy Acuña, *Occupied America: The Chicano's Struggle Toward Liberation* (San Francisco: Canfield Press, 1973), pg. 3.
15. Ibid., pg. 3f.

# The Humanization of Bilingual-Bicultural Schooling

**ERNESTO GALARZA**

Bilingual instruction has a long history in the United States. Its lessons are familiar to students of the subject. Among them are the following:

Where the home or ancestral language is not English, children who are first taught reading in that language (the first language of the child) will learn to read English better and more quickly. There is evidence to the effect that competence in reading in one language not only does not interfere with reading in another but tends to enhance it. The best medium for the initial states of learning, where such learning relies mainly on aural and verbal communication, is the child's dominant language.

These conclusions, based on past research and confirmed by current practice, make uncommonly good sense. Linguistic patterns are firmly fixed during the first four or five years of life. During that time they become a vital part of the psyche of the person, and they cannot be abandoned or proscribed without resistance by the individual. This means that he will be phychically disturbed rather than reassured by instruction presented to him in a language he does not understand. Furthermore, the transition from ability to hear and speak a language to reading it

---

These remarks on bilingual-bicultural education have been abstracted from a longer essay by Dr. Galarza entitled "Bilingual-Bicultural Education in the San José Unified School District." They are reproduced with the permission of the original publishers, the Department of Urban Education of the San José (California) School District and the San José Model Cities, Inc.—Editor.

takes far less effort than to master all three skills simultaneously in an unfamiliar language.

With these propositions in mind, it may be stressed that the home language, by its process of relatively free association, has in fact functioned positively in the growth and development of the child. This is because there is a direct and immediate connection between what the child experiences and what he hears and says. This spontaneity is not restrained by rules about the mechanics of speech, spoken or written. It is therefore, on the part of the child, an experience of success. Only later, much later, is the child able to understand intellectually that the mechanics of learning—phonics, grammar, syntax and the rest—are useful devices by which he can master more complicated areas of experience.

To these ends bilingual schooling has been defined as instruction in two languages and the use of both as mediums of instruction for any part or all of the school curriculum. The guidelines issued by the California State Department of Education under the ACT of 1972 adopt this definition.

Historical experience validates not only these concepts, but also the social and political and technical conditions upon which their success depends. The competence of teachers in the home language (in this case Spanish) must be of a high order. The administrators of the school system must give the bilingual program their support. The community must believe that bilingual instruction is beneficial. Parents must accept the view that the maintenance of the home language and the transfer to English do not raise an "either-or" dilemma, but are two complementary elements in the growth and development of the child.

## LANGUAGE MAINTENANCE AND LANGUAGE TRANSFER

Bilingual schooling offers a human and sensible answer to the linguistic problems of a child who is reared in one language and is suddenly plunged into a school world that teaches him in another. The psychological and pedagogical evidence goes from persuasive to convincing. The resistance that remains is not based on consideration, backed up by evidence, of child growth and development, but on contraposing the concepts of language maintenance and language transfer.

There is no doubt as to the roots of the concept of language maintenance. They are in the cultural survivals of ethnic minorities whose adults strongly desire and even demand that the "old country" traditions, mores, customs and traits, including speech, be imprinted on their young. Cultural heritage has been central to the demands of Mexican Americans for bilingual schooling. They have viewed it, as have all other ethnic minorities, as an important condition of restorint their prestige and status in the community at large.

The fact that cultural maintenance and linguistic loyalty have not been dramatically successful in the United States does not argue for underrating their influence in many communities. They account for much of the momentum toward bilingual schooling in the last ten years.

Language transfer, on the other hand, can have the effect, and has had it in the past, of polarizing opposition to bilingual instruction. The argument runs that since the child is destined to function in an English speaking society, the sooner he learns English the better. This position invites a cultural encounter with the language maintainers; and for this reason the more the issue is argued the more obscure the controversy becomes.

It is worth noting in this connection that the official position of the State of California, enacted by its legislature, is that, *from the standpoint of the child*, language maintenance and language transfer are both vital elements in his growth and development. This is not a crude political compromise but rather a legislative acknowledgement of the conditions of effective instruction for children who must negotiate a difficult cultural transition. For the very young learner, the maintenance of language is not an issue of sentimental ties with ancestors or a vital matter of ethnic prestige. It is a crucial condition of psychological stability, or personal psychic integration, under the most favorable conditions possible.

There is reason to believe that these conditions are also those that prepare the way for language transfer, which indeed also becomes a necessity for the child as he confronts his needs for getting along with multilingual peers and of making his way successfully through a second language and a second culture.

This is the course on which the schools of California are now launched: 1. to meet through bilingual instruction the linguistic needs of minority children whose first (family) language is not English; 2. to facilitate transfer to English of such children; and 3. to preserve and enhance linguistic skills acquired in the home.

Two important things should be noticed about the above statements. First, they reflect primarily and dominantly the point of view of the child as a growing and developing individual. Second, as a matter of official policy, is the question, whether, and how far and for how long the linguistic skills acquired in the family can be preserved and enhanced.

In this latter connection we must take into account that preservation and enhancement have important consequences for both the individual and for the community. The present shortage of U.S.-born teachers of Mexican ancestry who possess the high competence noted as one of the conditions of the success of bilingual instruction makes two points with one illustration. Mexican American teachers whose first (family) language was Spanish and whose skills thus acquired were not preserved or enhanced throughout their schooling, cannot compete in teaching effectiveness with Mexican-born and bred teachers and must go through time-consuming, arduous and expensive in-service training to so compete. This is a personal as well as a community loss, as evidenced by the difficulties that school systems are having in locating U.S.-born "Chicano" teachers with optimum competencies.

## THE PATTERN OF INSTRUCTION

Educational philosophies, methods and even techniques are the results of a political process that goes on continuously in the community among those adults who take an active interest and part in the schooling of the young. Except in rare instances, and only at the high school or college level, the young, as the objects of public schooling, are not the agents of change in philosophies, methods and techniques. They can manifest their needs, but not articulate them. An assessment of needs is an adult response to them and on the next higher level an articulation on behalf of the young of how to respond to the needs.

Here a word of caution is in order. The process of assessment and articulation is rarely clear cut and unambiguous. It is more often infiltrated by "needs" other than those of the young. There is the "need" of some parents to preserve the culture, and therefore the language, of a past recalled with affection. There is the "need" of persons who would find para-professional or professional employment in a bilingual program. There is the "need" of providers of instructional materials for which bilingual instruction would open new markets.

These are not "needs" but cultural and material expectations of certain sectors of the adult community. Whatever their legitimate role in the final decisions on educational policy, they are secondary to needs for growth and development of the child.

Once the linguistic needs of the children are found and instruction in a language other than English is approved, decisions have to be made in two major respects. The first question that arises is, how shall the available time for instruction be distributed between English and the first (home) language? The second, how shall the subject matter be allocated as between the two languages?

These distributions should not be arbitrary. They should reflect the linguistic condition of the learners at any given time. Clearly, for children who are completely monolingual in a language other than English, instruction, all instruction, can reach them only in their first (home) language. As their skills in English advance, more latitude is available for the distribution of time and subject matter. Such advancement will come by degrees, the guiding principle throughout being that no child shall be taught anything in a language he does not understand.

As the learner moves away from complete dependency on his home language, options more flexible and numerous are open to the school. It has been estimated that more than 250 combinations of time and subject matter are available, theoretically, to the curriculum planner of a bilingual program. (See William F. Mackey, *A Typology of Bilingual Education*, International Center for Research on Bilingual Education, Quebec, Canada.)

It is in the selection of the pattern that best suits the learners, that more genuinely reflects the cultural styles of the community and that better prepares the child to operate in those social universes which will be open to him, that the understanding and skill of the bilingual instructors are demonstrated. For instance, it has been pointed out that the kind and degree of language reinforcement which the child receives in the normal course of his life at home and in the community should figure heavily in the type of bilingual instruction to be given in the school. The talk of peers and of radio and television programs is only a part of the cultural situation that must be taken into account by the school. Communities differ importantly in this respect, and no bilingual program can be justified in the long run if it stands isolated from that situation. There are to be considered such factors as the ethnic distribution of the immediate community served by the school, the larger areas of contact of the individual, the cultural resources available to the family and used by its members, the ethnic ratios within the school itself, the numbers of speakers of the given language who are in active contact with one another in a locality.

## THE BILINGUAL CURRICULUM

Every innovation in schooling presents both a temptation and an opportunity. The innovation may be a philosophical approach, a method heretofore untried, a marked difference in curriculum design or a rearrangement of power and control of school policy. The temptation lies in the accommodation of what is offered as new to the vested requirements of what is old. The opportunity consists in recognizing potentials in the new that will make schooling progressively more responsive to the human condition of the child, past, present and future.

The traditional "curriculum" on which the bilingual program will be grafted stresses competitiveness and personal achievement. Textbook instruction determines the main tracks along which both methods and subject matter move. Cognition as a product measures achievement and rewards competitiveness. Reading skills and their attainment overpower and nearly banish other considerations. Verbal forms become practically the only sign language that is recognized as a means of communication. The whole schooling process, from kindergarten to graduate school, is motivated by expectations, increasingly postponed and rationalized by delayed rewards for personal competitive success.

It will be noticed that the word "curriculum" in the preceding paragraph is placed in quotation marks. By this it is intended to suggest that the curriculum which is being quoted is the traditional one, and that it is understood and practiced as a series of assignments of cognitive goals.

It would seem that the bilingual innovation could recognize that social awareness and group success are also important products of situations contrived to make instruction possible. Textbook time tables and schedules could be considered at best as main routes of learning open to innumerable feeder lines of unpredictable interests and spontaneous side trips into experience. Cognition could be regarded as the continuous activity of all the child's senses in the natural and social worlds that surround him, and that can be consciously made more sensitive, discriminating, and interactive. Reading skills could be properly placed within a more ample understanding of other vital skills necessary to a fully developing person. It could be recognized that those other skills, too, are different styles of communication, allowing the personality to express itself beyond the point where words fail. The whole instructional process, especially for young learners, could become less of a means to remote ends and more of a lively experience that is such because it is present, reassuring, and therefore an end in itself.

Because bilingual instruction is *bilingual* as a concept and as a description, it is particularly important for bilingual instructors to notice a difference between "curriculum" as a series of cognitive assignments and curriculum understood as a series of experiences carrying instructional values. These values are by no means exclusively linguistic. Ability to read is not the least of the products of schooling experiences, but it is not all.

Some of the overtones of curriculum understood in these terms can be briefly stated.

Education can be thought of as progress of the individual powered by his own experience, observation, feeling, thought, curiosity, and biological endowment, rather than as the power of adults over him. This is motivation in its genuine sense: the forward movement of personality towards enlarging cycles of experience anchored in a sense of worth and success in the past. It is the deeper meaning of being "turned on." Experience of this quality is a fine blend of the cognitive (ability to notice, recognize, and arrange real things); heuristic (the interest in pursuing knowledge beyond what is immediately obvious); creative (the joy of impressing upon an experience the stamp of the experiencing personality); expressive (the flow of spontaneity into the perpetual mix of the inner and outer worlds of the individual human life); affective (the exercise of emotion to establish healthy loyalties and psychological securities among peers); and social (the ability to recognize what the companionship of others provides and the willingness to accept its responsibilities along with its pleasures).

This is a somewhat lengthy definition of curriculum as a series of experiences, deliberately planned and provided by the

# HUMANIZATION OF SCHOOLING

educator, to promote the growth and development of the child, looking at him eventually as a member of a society. It means growth and development in the direction indicated by Piaget, "the increasing coherence of self and non-self;" man as a thing among things, as an event among events, as a person among persons. So that an assessment of needs, beginning with a technical inquiry about linguistic liabilities ends with a recognition of the "needs" of growth and development direction of all children.

It hardly requires special notice that cognitive skills and cognitive possessions are part and parcel of this whole process, not the least but also not all. Bilingual instruction cannot become an unreasonable claim that it will cure the defects of present public schooling. But by being sensed as one component of a new context, as an innovation, it can be an opportunity rather than a temptation.

## PHASING IN

The minimum conditions for introducing a bilingual instructional program include the following:

1. Completion of an assessment of needs based upon an approved procedure.
2. Appointment by the Board of Education of a director of bilingual instruction.
3. Negotiation of agreements or understanding with each school where bilingual instruction is requested.
4. Creation of an arrangement by which the District's supervisor of the program can maintain connection with the principal, teachers, and parents of children currently enrolled in bilingual classes.

These minimum conditions will merely initiate a process by which certain desirable characteristics will be brought into bilingual instruction at the level of each school. The needs assessment should eventually become a continuing procedure, familiar to the parents as well as to the administrators and teachers. These adults are the best informed sources on the prevailing culture and language of the neighborhood. A director can give bilingual instruction, indispensable administrative support and initiative. It is through an effective administrator that neighborhood points of view and values can be related to the broader uses and the wider horizons of bilingualism in contemporary life. What kinds of school district assistance each program is to receive and what responsibilities will be assumed by its administrators, teachers, and parents can be useful in two respects if they are reduced to agreements or understandings: one, they can apply past experience to the continuing program of instruction; and two, they can provide a basis for continuous review and adaptation to changing conditions. Programs will undoubtedly be revised from year to year. Between revisions there will be a regular interchange of information and evaluations between the director of the district program and the involved adult personnel of each school.

Considering that serious attention to the language handicaps of "minority" children were for so long ignored, it is not surprising that decisions are likely to be made out of sense of urgency, almost of crisis. The data from an assessment of needs should establish priorities as to types of children most urgently requiring help. Assistance to such children should come first; but over and beyond "crash" programs that mostly reflect past negligence on the part of school systems, it should be recognized that only persistent effort on plans carefully made can eventually produce successful bilingual instruction. Success would be evidenced by teachers who are highly competent in the use of Spanish, appropriate materials, adequate supportive services, cultural awareness, a curriculum that avoids boring the children in a first language as it often does in a second, and evaluation and testing procedures that are culturally compatible.

## IN-SERVICE TRAINING

Classroom teachers need retraining. In-service indicates that changes in instructional goals and values have occurred and that the new schooling performances required by such changes now make it necessary to send the teacher back to school.

Progress in any profession implies a growth of knowledge, replacement of old values by new ones, shifts of emphasis, formulation of concepts that serve the clients of the profession better, improvement of techniques, sometimes drastic reforms in methodology, and not infrequently radical departures in philosophy.

The problem is not how to slow down such growth to avoid the inconvenience of adjusting to it, but how to differentiate between substantive progress and modish behavior. The profession of schooling is singularly inclined to the latter. Instructional innovations can move quickly from hypothesis to proposition to promotion to catch-word to programming and thus to in-service training. Outwardly, something like this has happened to bilingual schooling. Those who find themselves disturbed or perturbed, unfamiliar or inadequate in bilingual instruction, are likely to be hoping that in the not very long run it will prove to be one of many of schooling's passing fancies.

Inwardly, however, bilingual-bicultural schooling has the potential of becoming a major and permanent advance for the United States society. This remains to be argued and proved convincingly, and to the extent that it is so proved it will require new skills, and indeed new attitudes of U.S. educators. It already has brought its own set of requirements for in-service training of teachers in bilingual schooling.

At the present time bilingual instruction is running a gamut of skeptical and even unfriendly, not to say hostile, appraisal. As indispensable as in-service training is, the conditions under which it is administered and even required can themselves diminish enthusiasm for bilingualism. In-service training for bilingual instruction is apt to be just one more "special program" attended outside the regular daily schedule and added to the already demanding requirement of the formal curriculum. Out-of-school meetings for orientation are apt to be called. Workshops can become another form of more work with less time to do it in. Through the mind of the teacher run serious professional questions: "How do I carry the new bilingual methods from in-service training into my class room? What kinds of materials will I need? Where can I get them? What should I read? Am I competent enough in Spanish?" Goals, objectives, aims, and values in bilingual instruction can be so new that the teacher feels as if facing something as drastic as a mental retreading or as awesome as a religious conversion. When the teacher is additionally considered as a spouse or a parent, bilingual instruction is not likely to stand very high in his or her priorities.

If bilingual-bicultural schooling is bringing new values and insights into U.S. schooling that will prove enduring, the possibility that it will some day be lightly discarded can be lessened by using in-service training in a manner that will not add to the already obvious strains of teaching. Better still, in a manner that will diminish those strains and thus become a factor in humanizing teaching as well as reading.

## PRE-SERVICE TRAINING

Essentially, in-service training is remedial. Since it now takes five years of college to certify a teacher, it may be assumed that it will take that long to graduate teachers who will have been prepared specifically for bilingual instruction. The aim is to avoid remedial retraining in the future, or at least to lay such adequate foundations in the preparation of teachers as will not require in the future such traumatic reconditioning as in-service training often entails.

It is in this connection especially that a Joint Bilingual Services Council can play an extremely useful role. Pre-service courses should be conceived and organized with continuing awareness of what other agencies and other programs are experiencing in this field. Insofar as the Mexican child is concerned, these courses must deal with his ancestral history and culture, the experience of his own group and his first language, Spanish. They must also incorporate the results of fifty years of research on child growth and development. It may even be possible, if pre-service training answers to its responsibilities, that the financing, administration, philosophy, design, and practice of U.S. schooling, by way of bilinguistic, bicultural innovations can change the concept of the teacher in the class. In place of the driven drudge of classroom routine, special programs, accountability, and in-service fringe penalties, the teacher might become the respected strategist of the growth and development of the children entrusted to her by a community and a system ready to act in her support.

## AIDES IN BILINGUAL INSTRUCTION

The use of aides in the classroom has become a part of bilingual practice in school districts with large enrollments of Spanish-speaking children. They are employed in the San José District and they are likely to become a permanent part of the administrative plan of bilingualism. Because of their numbers and their presence in the classroom, aides should receive more consideration under the heads of pre- and in-service training than they have in the past. Unless assigned as a mere flunky to the teacher and content to remain in that status, the aide enters increasingly into the instructional process. Awareness of instructional problems grows, and observation of teaching situations develops a consciousness of role that must be positively clarified and guided.

There has been enough experience with the aides system to indicate that such clarification and guidance should be provided more systematically than in the past. In-service training can be required of aides after they are hired, and pre-service orientation before. Such training deserves particular attention in bilingual programs. Generally speaking, aides operate uncertainly either as assistant housekeepers or sub-professionals. If bilingual schooling is to use them more and more in the latter category, their sub-professional training should be taken seriously by administrators. Who is to offer such training? What is it to consist of? How can it be designed so that it offers genuine instructional insights?— These are questions that must be posed and answered more deliberately than they have in the past. The professional, ethical and administrative issues raised by the use of aides can hamper bilingual instruction in subtle as well as noticeable ways if they are not resolved constructively.

## COMPETENCIES IN SPANISH

If bilingual schooling is to justify the funds and the effort spent on it, teacher competency in the language other than English must be judged by increasingly higher standards. A rising level of expectations as to what a bilingual teacher ought to know and be able to do is necessary if the low benchmark from which they have started is to be raised. That requirements for assignment of a teacher to a bilingual class have been less than strict can be admitted without embarrassment. In less than a decade school systems had to be turned around to qualify for federal and state funding of massive bilingual programs. In some respects this has called for drastic changes in attitudes and improvisations of many sorts, ranging from statements of instructional philosophy to design and production of materials. Not the least of these improvisations has occurred in the matter of teaching personnel.

So far as the teaching of Spanish in bilingual programs is concerned, the start was not auspicious. In states like California, it was conditioned by generations of neglect or hostility on the part of the official establishment, which did not concern itself with respecting or preserving or enhancing the language skills of Mexican, Spanish-speaking children. Their culture faded, and their Spanish skills were leached through official indifference and neglect. It is from their ranks that much of the recruiting of bilingual teachers has had to be done.

It is no offense to the ethnic ego or to the educator's pride to confess all this. The important thing is to recognize that under these historical circumstances improvisation is unavoidable, but also that it is provisional. It should not be too much to hope that within ten years the present incompetencies will be leveled upward. This can be done partly through in-service training but mainly through pre-service training. The competencies to be considered relate to knowledge of the Spanish language and skills in using it. They also have to do with a wide curriculum of cultural matters of which the current language of Mexican communities is a part.

## PARENT PARTICIPATION

It is one of the tenets of bilingual instruction that parents shall have the opportunity to take part in the entire process. This begins with the choice as to whether or not children will be enrolled in bilingual classes. For those parents who approve, the schools are expected to offer opportunities for involvement. Involvement has taken a number of forms. Parents have been appointed to advisory committees which pass on matters of policy. The schools are expected to encourage demonstrations of cultural skills by parents in the classroom. The prevailing view appears to be that parents should know what is going on in the school and to have the opportunity to express themselves about it.

This desirable aspect of bilingual, bicultural schooling could be made more effective if parental roles were somewhat more specifically described and presented as options to the parents. These are some of the ways in which this might be done: identification of adults who have a craft or other skills they are willing to demonstrate in classrooms; lectures in Spanish to explain the methods and philosophy of current instruction; consultation of parents in a continuing assessment of needs based on a procedure established by the school district; presentation of visual programs about classroom activities illustrating what the school is doing and why; convocation of discussion groups to provide facts and elicit opinions whenever a situation or issue arises that commands the present interest of the community of parents; a service of technical information for parents who are members of advisory committees and who as such are called upon to make policy judgements.

While the doors to participation should be kept open to all parents, it is not likely that most of them will be prompted to participate actively on the level of a general interest in the schooling progress of the school system as a whole. It is probable that they will be more interested in the instructional experiences of their own children in the specific classes in which they are enrolled. If this is true, it might be desirable to organize that local interest into supportive and informational committees identified specifically with particular classes. The local interest could then be personalized by identifying organized parents with their own children in their own class. In this way important decisions which are now made by the school alone could be explained and used to promote the schooling of the parents themselves.

There is another, more productive use of class committees of this type—to apply them to the encouragement of activities supporting what the bilingual teacher is trying to do in the classroom. Being read to at home strengthens the effect of being read to at school. But in many instances the parents would require and perhaps welcome guidance in reading techniques as well as assistance in providing the home with reading material complementary to those of the school.

Parent participation implies the assumption by parents of certain responsibilities, like reading at home, that can encourage responsiveness of the school and the family to each other and the child to both. There are precise technical methods to be worked out to accomplish this; the class committees can be a means to identify and apply them. Compared to other forms of parent participation, this seems to offer the most immediate benefits for children receiving bilingual instruction.

## COMMUNITY INVOLVEMENT

Community involvement in the school, like parent participation, is a characteristic of bilingual-bicultural schooling. Since without its presence it is not likely that a school district will obtain federal or state funding for bilingual programming, it can be described as a required characteristic. It can be argued that there is a difference between the two concepts. Parent participation, as suggested above, should aim at increasing closeness of the family and the school on the level of the growth and development of the individual child and the enlistment of the support of the family itself in encouraging that development. Community involvement, on the other hand, supposes a more general interest in the operation of the school system as a whole in the cultural and linguistic areas. This, in turn, presupposes that there is in the community a structure or ways and means by which that general interest can be expressed, by which it can ask questions and consider the answers and make suggestions as to policies.

If such a structure does not exist, if such ways and means are absent, the school district itself must give thought to creating them and making them viable.

## EVALUATION AND RESEARCH

Advisory bodies and consultative committees very soon fall into disuse unless they are genuinely functional within the system. Two important functions which the council could assume would be research and evaluation. As to research, the object would be to assemble data related to the progress of the bilingual-bicultural program in meeting the needs of Spanish speaking children. The assessment of needs should be continuing, technically reliable, and adequately reported to the school authorities and the community. The advisory council can be the channel for this.

As a function of the advisory council, the same objective would apply with regard to evaluation. The evaluative process should be as continuous as possible, with the teachers and parents as participants as well as all those staff members who are responsible for day-to-day operation of the program. Special advisers could be contracted from time to time to provide professional judgements when needed; but the aim should be to evaluate the action as it unfolds, and its purpose should be the recognition of successful action as well as the correction of mistakes, oversights, laxity, or unproductiveness.

## RESOURCE STAFF

A bilingual-bicultural program for a district with ongoing activities on various fronts and at different levels and calling for active participation by family and community will require effective supportive services. At whatever point of the district's administrative machinery they are attached, these services are important to keep the numerous participants in the total program moving forward together.

In any public program of any proportion there is much that can become esoteric and even mystifying if there is not within it an adequate exchange system of information and services. It is not possible to answer all the questions, provide for all the contingencies, coordinate all the resources, and anticipate all the needs in advance. Provided the goals are clearly stated and the commitments are taken seriously, creative team operation will be possible, even among a comparatively large number of persons. The two requirements are clear definition of responsibilities and ways and means to bring guidance and help to those in the program who need to know and to act. These needs are particularly important in the parent and community sector of the program. If rigidity is to be avoided in bilingual-bicultural instruction, the traffic of ideas, information, materials, equipment, and insights will have to be lively and responsive.

Like the use of aides, parent participation and community involvement resource services must be particularized and special staff training for them provided.

## CONCLUSION

An adequate bilingual-bicultural program must concern itself with materials, teacher training, language skills, parent participation, community involvement, curriculum strategies, educational philosophy, and cultural awareness. From time to time the emphasis may shift from one of these areas to another, but over time the program must advance evenly on all fronts. Neglect of any of them will unbalance the whole effort.

Special attention should be given to the aspect of culture because it is the area least clearly defined at the present time and most likely to contain vague concepts and blurred objectives. It is important to avoid these faults since they can reverse priorities and derail the activities of the participants, possibly creating false expectations in the community and missing the central purposes of so much effort and expense.

These purposes, in order of priority, would appear to be as follows.

*Number one:*
to prevent the injury done to young learners who are compelled to take instruction in language they do not understand, or in which they have limited skills.

*Number two:*
> to reinforce and to encourage the feeling of self-significance socially and self-worth psychologically by recognizing and respecting the culture into which the child is born.

*Number three:*
> to preserve and enhance the language skills which the child acquires in the culture of his birth without interfering with other linguistic skills that will prepare him to act in the second culture that will condition his future life.

*Number four:*
> to provide the child, in the fulfillment of these priorities, with a continuing series of school and home experiences in all of which there are always present the following vital elements—cognitive growth, interest aroused by the significance to the learner of what he is learning, creative use of things and situations, spontaneity in his responses which will bring the element of delight into learning, affection for things learned and for the persons with whom they are learned, and ability to give and receive companionship among peers.

The cultural content of a bilingual program should serve these primary ends, not be dominated by them. If they are clearly stated and conscientiously pursued, the element of condescension toward minorities will be discouraged; for it will be seen that what society is doing is not so much treating the individuals as curing itself. Here the so-called Anglo culture and the so-called Mexican meet on common ground. Both will have to look at themselves in critical evaluation of how far they serve and to what extent they fail with respect to primary ends.

The child is entitled to these priorities. They are the foundations for an adult life that is capable of reshaping society in significant ways so that it better serves the ends of humanity itself.

# Three Intellectuals: Justo Sierra, Trinidad Sánchez Santos, Ricardo Flores Magón

## JUAN GÓMEZ-QUIÑONES

John Friedmann argues persuasively that intellectuals, not only economic entrepreneurs or political office holders, are agents in precipitating change.[1] Intellectuals contribute to social change in the realm of values and ideas. Friedmann concisely states the functions of the innovating intellectual:

> The functions of intellectuals in societies undergoing radical transformation from a traditional-agrarian to a progressive-urban pattern of living are many and significant. Choices between traditional and modern values must be clarified; old traditions must be reinterpreted according to the spirit of the times; new ideas must be tied into a meaningful pattern of historical relationships; new ideological weapons must be shaped; and the meaning of national culture and destiny must be redefined. In short, the intellectuals must exhort, inform, interpret, and idealize. The economic and social changes that concurrently go on are only rendered possible as a sustained and continuing process by the constant barrage of words that intellectuals let loose upon their fellow citizens. All the strains, tensions, hopes, frustrations, conflicts, and feelings of exuberance that usually accompany a period of rapid social change will be discovered in their purest, most intensive form among them.[2]

George Sánchez was part of a historical tradition of Mexican intellectuals who have worked to bring about social change. Justo Sierra, Trinidad Sánchez and Ricardo Flores Magón were three Mexican intellectuals who contributed to promoting change and arousing national consciousness. Each was representative of a sector of the national community and each influenced his times. Certainly none was *the* voice or represented all the nation or in his thought expressed all the aspirations, concerns, and eventual solutions. However, each shaped public thinking and influenced political decisions. Their ideas contributed to national goals, popular values and institutions. Among the three there was diversity, contradiction and unity. They interpreted the past, scrutinized the present, and advocated a particular future. They also clearly mirrored the consciousness and anxiety of the period.

## JUSTO SIERRA-MÉNDEZ

Justo Sierra-Méndez was a man of singular worth both as an ideologist and an educator, significant not only as a writer and speaker but important also for his active political participation, and direct administrative responsibilities.[3] He was uniquely respected in national circles. In his makeup one trait is clear. Explicitly, Sierra was passionately devoted to the greatness of the patria. This devotion was rooted in idealism yet was pragmatically and rationally approached. It was practiced principally in three fields: politics, history, and education.

With the reinstatement of the Liberal government in 1867, Sierra received recognition through his poetry and radical liberal fervor which gained him access to the circles of Altamirano and other Juaristas. Though he delayed completing his law degree, he received it in 1871.

In the 1860s and 1870s his principal activities were in literature and journalism. From 1868 through 1880 Sierra wrote commentary in the prominent Liberal newspapers of the day: *El Globo, El Siglo XIX, El Federalista, El Bien Público*, eventually co-founding the seminal newspaper, *La Libertad*. He had a circle and a public. He met Juárez on several occasions and was deeply impressed, listening carefully to the President's suggestion that he take a greater interest in politics. Taking the advice, he was elected to congress from Veracruz. It marked a new step.

In his youth, Sierra was an ardent Liberal of the "escuela metafísica," as he would later label it.[4] He revered the Liberals of the Reform. Uncritically he accepted their ideals, their beliefs in a republican democratic government and the viability of the Constitution of 1857. Growing maturity, the death of Juárez, disillusionment with the venality in the practice of law, and political experiences all influenced the turn in Sierra's life in the mid-seventies. In 1875, in a polemic with Gabino Barreda, he began to define an independent position separate from the extreme Liberals, the Comtists and Conservatives.[5] He re-evaluated his political beliefs and through analysis defined a new position, one that was his own. In so doing, he influenced many of his fellow citizens. This new direction suggests the import and assimilation of ideas stemming from the writings of Spencer, Darwin, Mills, and other Europeans.

Sierra's views and criticisms on the Constitution of 1857 were the touchstone of many of his political ideas; they led to suggested reforms.[6] He defined, in effect, a mid-position between Liberals and Conservatives and polemicized against both. Conservatism was retrogressive; the other was anarchical.

For the absolute necessities of national unification and progress which were, in turn, national salvation he proposed rational politics, and realistic compromises. Experience dictated, Sierra advised, support of the existing administration, a more careful definition of civil liberties, a stronger executive, and for assurance, an independent judiciary, a reconstituted Senate, and the organization of a government party. In the nonpolitical spheres he pressed for scientific studies to better guide policy, for establishment of communication systems, for foreign investment, credit and tax systematization, free trade, European colonization, obligatory education, and a vigorous educational effort—all intended to strengthen México. To those that measure politics by absolute moral axioms, there was in his propositions a certain amount of cynicism and elitism. Yet from the first he cautioned that all government policy must rest on education and justice or it will be bankrupt.[7]

In the pages of *La Libertad*, Sierra defined the new position Liberal-Conservador.[8] The position had general premises and specific application; in effect it was premised on an historical analysis, a scientific method; it preserved Liberal humanitarian ideals and had as its moral standard utilitarianism. Thus he pinned his hopes for the realization of his ideals on evolution because to him revolution and anarchy were retrogressive.[9] He saw society as an organism in constant evolution. Progress was determined according to the extent that the internal energy of any given society permits progress to dominate and assimilate external elements, thus insuring the development of that society.[10]

Accordingly, the individual, through the aid of science, must ascertain the actual evolutionary state of society and must scientifically endeavor to realize to the fullest the potentialities of that stage. The full realization of one stage leads naturally to the next. In the process the individual must keep in mind the eventual goals of justice, freedom and liberty. Thus the individual must be both an idealist and a realist; and in order to maintain progress with order, be both a liberal and a conservative. This meant that the individual had to do what was needed for the realization of the transcendence of the present evolutionary state, regardless of personal consideration. Politically it meant serving the state for national development; however, the service was not contingent on personal endorsement of all the governing processes. Given the reality of México at the time, it was a salutary and modern advocation.

México needed stability and peace in order to attempt material progress which would enable social progress to take place. Sierra premised his political position on the view of society as a continual developmental process with certain general "stages" and "laws." In this process, evolutionary change was identified as the most progressive, while revolution was viewed as abnormal and counter-progressive. Sierra held that individual rights were determined by utility to the progressive interests of humanity; civil rights were not absolute. The State, if need be, should function with authority and conservativism, though justice must not be disregarded. This was necessary to achieve the goals of a democratic, free, and prosperous society. The call was for harsh realism in politics for the sake of progress.

Sierra, again elected to Congress in 1880 from a district in Sinaloa, distinguished himself even more than before as a legislator. He presented legislation on educational reform, archaeological conservation, a national commemoration, and national finances. The last became unpleasantly controversial. He supported payment of the debt to Great Britain, a long-standing Mexican obligation, including the loans contracted by the non-Liberal government. This was very unpopular. Acknowledgement was necessary for the strengthening of México's international and financial position. Sierra supported the González administration's recognition of the debt because credit was indispensable for rebuilding the economy and European credit was especially needed to avoid total dependency on American financing.[11] To Sierra, it was pragmatic politics, unpleasant but required.

Through the 1880s and 1890s he was active in Congress where he was part of a small group that endeavored to introduce reforms generally discussed years earlier in the late seventies. From one perspective, this work culminated in the Convención del Partido Liberal in 1892. The discussions and the platform reflected the extent to which the ideas preached originally in *La Libertad* were part of the public domain.[12] It was an attempt, to be sure, to provide legitimacy for Díaz' reelection, but also to provide a rational program to guide, to broaden, and to define the regime. Sierra was a key figure in this.

Sierra's political analysis and political solutions, his premises and reforms, were the substance of the *Manifiesto de la Convención Nacional Liberal* of 1892. The *Manifiesto* encompassed but also broadened public opinion. Sierra's ideas provided the Díaz regime with an intellectual rationale, which was a pragmatic neo-Liberalism that defined its means and goals in the slogan "orden y progreso."

In 1892, the basic outlines of the earlier program were visible: peace, communications, abolishment of internal tariffs, closely defined freedoms, statistical studies, popular education, and an independent judiciary. In regard to the *Convención* of 1892 Sierra intended a program and a political party to guide the latitude of government in the absence of a visible electorate. As the years went by he maintained these views but with apparent apprehension. He visibly lost enthusiasm for foreign colonization, free trade, and foreign investment. He realized that these did not serve México's development. Also noticeable was the growing concern for social dissatisfaction and the denial of civil liberties, as well as apprehension for the continuing need for reelection. Though at one time he had supported U.S. investment, he eventually lost his enthusiasm for it and in addition grew alarmed over the United States' cultural influence.[13]

The acceptance of Díaz, a phenomenon he apparently had seen originally as transitory, had been one of Sierra's first demonstrable compromises.[14] He endorsed Díaz and was proud to be his collaborator, though this obviously did not mean endorsement or complicity in all acts of the regime.[15] In 1892 the dictatorship was still a fact of political life and generally seen as beneficent, though only on certain conditional grounds. In 1899,

Sierra rather pointedly wrote to Díaz stating his doubts concerning the long term results of reelection.[16] Sierra had in fact accepted a dictatorship and had advocated its acceptance, but with a greater insistence had maintained that complete democracy was an eventual goal of the present economic development with an educational system, laying the foundations. Sierra threaded a very thin line in politics.

In his profession as historian and as educator, his contributions were on firmer ground.[17] Long active in journalism and politics, Sierra gained prominence in the profession he took up after law, history. Upon the retirement of Altamirano, who had occupied the Chair of History at the Escuela Nacional Preparatoria, the then highest academic forum, Sierra accepted the position. To satisfy what he considered a dire need in 1877 and 1878, he prepared a text on general ancient history, his first major historiographical effort. His rigorous attention to fact, his wide use of sources and his attractive interpretation, marked the text as a highlight in Mexican historiography.

Justo Sierra indelibly stamped Mexican historiography; he provided a framework, an analysis for national history, and gave it a sense of purpose and a social function. The development of a positive view of national history and its dissemination is an important process of nationalism. What Sierra did now seems so obvious and so familiar that upon first encounter it is not readily perceivable, unless there is familiarity with what previously passed for professional history and what were the common popular notions of history. Incredibly, until the late nineteenth century, there were few writings that could be used as texts and often national history was not explicitly granted a place in the curriculum.

For Sierra, Mexican historiography had many problems and he urged their solution. He decried the absence of monographs, and he felt strongly the need for the compilation of statistics and the collection of documents. He asserted that whole periods or topics in national history were relatively unknown.[18] A major fault Sierra noted was the polemical quality of literature which in addition to its uselessness in the presentation of facts also markedly contributed to social divisiveness. Sierra, as much as was possible given the times, stressed strict professionalism in history, contributed to the body of literature and provided support for others working in the fields of history. Most important, he stressed continuity, equanimity, and harmony in the interpretation of history. He stressed understanding, not condemnation; he sought to extenuate failures and errors so that a historical harmony and concord might be visible.[19] Nonetheless, for him, history presented grounds for judgment, and the historian should offer judgment, though he ought not indulge in retrospective speculations.[20] He wanted, above all, to make patent the continuous repetition of error and loss of energy that Mexican history recorded.[21]

These admonishments, suggestions, and advocations were presented within his projection of a historical framework. He presented his courses and his texts in a setting of Western and American history. He developed and wrote a text, which was in essence one on Western civilization beginning with the earliest of recorded times. From that base he dealt with a presentation of a history of the Americas, "Latin" and "Anglo." Within this context he then proceeded to teach and present Mexican history.[22]

The larger framework for Mexican history which Sierra presented was one now rather familiar: Pre-Colombian Civilizations and the Conquest; the Colonial period and Independence; and the Republic, or National period. In approaching National history he made a number of divisions and subdivisions: 1. the subperiod of 1825-1848 (which was further divided into the Empire, 1821-1823; Federation and Militarism 1823-1835; and Centralism 1835-1848); 2. the period of the Reform, 1848-1867 (which was divided into "Reorganization and Reaction," 1848-1857; the Three Years War, 1858-1860; Intervention, 1861-1867); and 3. the contemporary period which began with 1867. In his view, the three major periods in national history were Independence, which inaugurated national life; the Reform, which established the "social character" of the nation; and the present period de la Paz, which defined the "international character" of the country.[23]

Understandably, history for him was the central discipline in the curriculum and the base for the others.[24] He advocated and instructed that history be taught from primary school on through to the higher levels. Most important for him, history provided the understanding which could make possible the transcendence of the past and the present stage; it also instilled pride, projected national ideals and cemented national unity. Sierra provided a national history that did just that, and thereby contributed to nationalism.

In the matter of history, as Sierra taught it, the historian and the educator were inseparable. His judgment of the national past and character was severe but his message was optimistic: if corrections take place, the future will be a prosperous one.[25] He held the mestizo as the one element in the population that was dynamic and the one from which national characteristics crystallized as Creoles and Indians were absorbed. The Indian was the principal problem; he must be recognized historically and as a fellow citizen. His standard of living and education must be raised and he must be incorporated into the nation. Despite the general bourgeois snobbishness of the times, Sierra's sense of community was inclusive; he stressed the idea of pueblo and identification with it. There was always patent in his thought a tolerance and pragmatism underpinning his central motives of instilling citizenship, sobriety, dedication to national welfare, and the fostering of pride and unity.

To illustrate graphically the values he sought to instill, Sierra focused on national heroes and holidays. Both were central didactic touchstones, serving unifying and emulative functions. To this end, as a young publicist and later as a congressman, he proposed a set of national holidays and argued that civic festivities should reflect the needs and participation of the people and not as self-serving stages for bureaucrats and bourgeoisie.[26] He sought legislation for his proposals which, among other aspects, called for a national pantheon which would be a visible shrine for civic devotion in the name of men who in any field had contributed to the nation. In later life he stressed the use of heroes in educating children and stressed the educational use of civic ceremonies.

Some of Sierra's most moving orations and writings were on themes provided by national heroes. In these, emphasis was placed on sacrifice and devotion for national welfare; the virtues highlighted were intelligence, dedication, and valor. He held Juárez in highest esteem. He saw him as an ideal object-lesson to counter the many failings to which Mexicans were prone.[27]

Significantly, Justo Sierra was elected in 1889 by assembled delegates to preside over the first National Congress on Public Instruction. For him, the immediate task was unification of elementary education on the policy basis of it being obligatory, secular, and free.[28] Sierra held that it was necessary to understand the functions of "education" versus "instruction." The latter accomplished the formation of complete men for the needs of the time and the country; the former energized, through the presentation of knowledge, the movement that would improve the present circumstances. He said that both had to be joined in the schools— the moral and the scientific, the utilitarian and altruistic.

Again elected to preside over the Second Congress on Public Instruction (January 20, 1891-February 28, 1891), Sierra presented a view of the state as the representative organ of all the society's common interests, the organ of the whole.[29] The state, accordingly, was within the social organism but had a life distinct from individual interests. It was judge and guardian, it performed inspection and maintained vigilance. Most important for education, it had the additional responsibility of civilizador, that is, promoter and coordinator for progress with its principal agency, the educational system.[30] Again, he insisted, education must join the ideal and the pragmatic, the theoretical and the practical in order to form a force that would change the present negative national situation for the better. He singled out for particular focus the redemption of the Indian to whom so much was owed and who possessed untold and unrealized potentialities.[31] For Sierra, the incorporation of the Indian was mandatory for achieving national unity and maximum strength.

At this important convention he advised the assembled delegates that their task as educators was the regeneration of the moral fiber of the Mexicans. Educators must inculcate some notions of civic responsibility to citizens who as yet did not have them, and make available to a wide sector, in a more defined, positive, and racially inclusive manner, the idea of nacionalidad in a very heterogeneous community. For the present, said Sierra, these assignments were the work of a minority because that was all that was available and could be made available. Thus, he felt, not for snobbish but for practical reasons, the first accomplishment was to train teachers, in the broad sense of the word, for a national educational system.[32]

Though Sierra's concern for education dates from his earliest years, it was in the period 1889-1911 that he defined and expanded his thoughts most fully. For an intellectual, Sierra was presented with an uncommon opportunity for putting his ideas into operation; first in his position as Sub-Secretary (1904) and later that of Secretary of Education (1909). He became an educator on a national scale, impressing his ideas on his contemporaries and on the twentieth century. Sierra brought to the task a global conception for an educational system and the dedication of a zealot. The purposes of education were to "crear el alma nacional" and to accelerate the material, intellectual, and moral progress of the nation. This was possible because education directly influenced individuals. "Educación mejora la acción, mejorando el agente."[33] His projection included pre-school to University, urban and rural, youth as well as adult education.

> . . . la escuela, esa es la immensa iglesia nueva, esa es la clave del porvenir.[34]

To Sierra, school was a means of attaining liberty. School was the key to avoid the repetition of historical mishaps and the best defense against foreign economic and cultural influences.

As Sierra developed his educational program, there were a number of sub-points within that are of interest. He favored education of women for the professions and the home, though advising them to stay out of politics.[35] As minister, he pioneered in the study and preservation of Indian archaeology. At one time he had seen no danger in the exodus of treasures to Europe, but by 1900 he was emphatic about their preservation and study in México, which signalled a cultural nationalism.[36] Sierra maintained that education had to be accomplished with enthusiasm, faith, and love, not merely with bureaucratic rules and technical expertise, and always with the idea that "por la patria, siempre por la patria todo."[37] Certainly Sierra's proudest educational accomplishment was the inauguration of the University in 1910, his project since the 1880s. It would crown and direct the educational system; it would be the center for learning and teaching, and also would aid in the strengthening of national character by placing each branch of knowledge within a Mexican context, "mexicanizar la ciencia."

On September 13, 1910, Sierra read a paper titled "La conquista de la patria por la educación," which was perhaps the most lucid and condensed expression of his thought on education, though it was not without a certain melancholy tone.[38] The plea was familiar: unity, moral strength, defense of national sovereignty, the sacred trust of teachers, and the goal of liberty and justice. The unstated, philosophic premise seemed to be that the individual could fully realize himself only through mergence with the larger national society; and only to the extent that the society had achieved its full potential, could the individual achieve this. To Sierra, the word "patria" encompassed all abstractions, all values, all ideals, but it was not above "la verdad" or "la humanidad."[39]

Justo Sierra exhibited nationalism and contributed to the nationalist process. His personal sense of community was inclusive, if somewhat paternal, and he advocated nationalism as a guiding spirit, ethos, in all activities and it was his basic motivation. His view of history stressed unity and continuity from the Indian past to the present. He also saw it as a socializing element. In education, his motives were the further greatness and progress of the nation. Sierra believed in a strong and active state. Though not extreme, he viewed with concern foreign influence in economics and culture. For him, the highest interests were those of the nation. Sánchez Santos agreed with him, only he viewed things from a conservative perspective rather than a liberal and his view of the national interest was religious as well as secular.

## TRINIDAD SÁNCHEZ SANTOS

"Por la religión y por la Patria," his chosen motto, synthesized the guiding ethos of Trinidad Sánchez Santos, foremost Catholic publicist during the years 1890-1911.[40] Though at present not often remembered, in his day he was a man of wide public influence because of his well-received writings, his gift as an orator, his newspaper, and the respect his integrity and well-known independence commanded, both from sympathizers and antagonists.[41] Sánchez Santos was a lay apostle, a crusader dedicated to the greatness of México and to the re-Catholization of México. Sánchez Santos represented Catholic social and political criticism of the society and the regime. He apparently did not see these as contradictory even though religion and the nation claim complete loyalty. He was a fervent Catholic and patriot. For him, the well-being and greatness of the nation and the cause of religion were intertwined. This was how he avoided the contradictions of two supreme loyalties. Luís Íslas García wrote:

> Sánchez Santos representa la parte de los católicos en la revolución, en la oposición a los errores del régimen liberal de don Porfirio; representa la lucha de las escencias nacionales contra la deformación de la dictatura. Sánchez Santos representa la defensa de los derechos de los humildes en una sociedad en que éstos carecían de voces que los defendieran.[42]

Sánchez Santos' professional career may be divided into three phases: the first, from 1879-1884, marked the years of apprenticeship as a journalist, closing with a series of incisive and satirical pieces on the English debt which gained major attention for him; the second period (1885-1898) included his years as a popular writer for several newspapers and his first failure at establishing his own publication; the period of maturity and apogee

(1899-1912) began with the publishing of *El País*, his own newspaper, and closed with his death; it was the period of direct and explicit forward-looking social and political criticism. From the beginning of his career he had been a political commentator, but in his early periods he was charming though sometimes caustic. More often than not his issues were moral and religious and he wrote historical defensive essays upholding the Catholic-Conservative side on past events. In his later years he added social criticism to his political commentary and proposed reforms for the future. In 1896 he said,

> El ataque a los errores sociales es un deber de la conciencia, un apostolado al patriotismo.[43]

The change he underwent is parallel with the noticeable alteration of the milieu in México at the time. He communicated his views through his newspaper, *El País*.

*El País* became a major newspaper rivaling *El Imparcial*, and went from a circulation of a few thousand to the remarkable figure of over 200,000 in its last two years.[44] It was a fine newspaper, with an attractive layout presenting excellent news coverage, both national and international, utilizing regular reporters and correspondents, and providing an excellent feature section. It was, indeed, the best newspaper of the times and a high point in Mexican journalism. In addition to his work as a publisher, Sánchez Santos was one of the best orators in his day and much in demand as a public speaker.

Sánchez Santos was an idealist, that is, he was concerned with spiritual reality—for him that reality should be the focus of man's endeavor. Sánchez Santos believed that the malaise of man was primarily spiritual and ideological. From these stem the injustice and imperfection apparent in society. A fervent Catholic and patriot, the question of religion and fatherland were integral to his actions and ideas. His own obsession with charity and justice, because they were Christian imperatives, his earnest desire for the revigorization and eventual greatness of México, and, of course, the times in which he lived, were to determine that he would become more specific and more progressive in what he advocated.

Sánchez Santos held an apocalyptic vision of his times. It was an era of crisis; he saw an impending doom for his country and religion. The view was couched in moral terms, though in the final decade it was extended to include economic-political perspective. Much of the fervor and anxiety in his writings, and especially in his speeches, stemmed from his belief. For him, the contest was between the forces of evil and those of salvation. México was a major battleground and Mexicans had a special stake in the battle; the major issue was morals. Hence vice and virtue are constants in his writings. He had three major themes: religious polemic, social-political criticism, and patriotic exhortation. His ideal was the realization of justice for the spiritual and material salvation and greatness of his country.

The Church was seen by Sánchez Santos as the preeminent social institution. Ideally, in a society universally and consciously Catholic and Christian, morals and values of that society would determine a benign operation of the State; the State would be a reflection of that society; there would be no church-state conflict. The form of government mattered little. However, Sánchez Santos was a confirmed democrat and social reformer.

On history, heroes, and symbols, Sánchez Santos shared Conservative bias except in his view of past Indian civilizations. He had no patience with historians who degraded the pre-Colombian Indian civilization, though admitted that there were those who exaggerated its virtues and accomplishments.[45] In his judgment, to deny their merits was an indulgence in "anti-mejicanismo." Understandably, what he found attractive in Indian civilization was the religiosity in all aspects of life and the high sense of morals, coupled with austere discipline and intense energy. He felt Mexicans could do well to emulate the virtues of the ancient civilizations. He always encouraged a proud appreciation of Indian cultures.[46] This led him to believe that the greatest debt was owed to the Indian in terms of heritage and labor contribution from time immemorial to the present. He argued that the Colonial period was the formative one in the social molding of the Mexican nation. In this, the Church played a major and beneficent role. It mitigated the harshness of the Conquest and brought Catholicism to México, which in turn led to the basis for future unity. Without the work of the Church, the incorporation of Indian and European would have been longer and more subject to animosity. The incorporation also included the amalgamation of previously divided Indian peoples. This view of the Colonial period did not make Sánchez Santos a rabid, hispanophile as was the case, for the most part, with Conservative writers.

The national symbols he preferred were the Virgen de Guadalupe and the national anthem. In rapturous rhetorical prose he eulogized the virtues of each. What he stressed most in both was that they were symbols, both meaningful and accessible, uniting to all. The Virgen was of prime importance to him as *the* Catholic, nationalistic, and continuing preeminent symbol to Mexicans over the years:

> Guadalupe: tu nombre y tu historia son como el silabario de nuestro patriotismo.[47]

For Sánchez Santos, the Virgen, God-given and uniquely Mexican, was the figurative expression of religion and patria. As an Indian-Mexican symbol, it evoked the past, while offering the promise for a great future.

On the speaker's forum or in articles, his efforts were toward defending the Church's role, especially in regard to the Indian and in vindicating Conservative heroes and actions during the nineteenth century. For him, the reforms of Charles II truncated Mexican historical evolution; from that point Mexicans had been alienated from their natural development.[48] The reforms weakened the Church, the constituent fiber of the nation. Sánchez Santos endorsed independence. The statesmanship of Iturbide was a sound attempt at avoiding anarchy and it was he who was the father of the country. In Sánchez Santos' historical analysis, Liberalism and its adherents had done incalculable harm to México by forcing adoption of political forms it could not fulfill, thereby endangering its future. Naturally he rejected the charge that the Conservatives had been traitorous during the American and French wars, though he did not endorse the Empire. He was a critic of the Díaz regime for its lack of a social policy and its negation of democracy. Through the 1880s and 1890s he was much concerned with history, though visibly less so in the last decade of his life when contemporary problems absorbed most of his attention.

In 1889 Sánchez Santos clearly stated that the fundamental task in politics for him was the "constituting" of the nation, by which he meant that the civic-political duty was to make law effective.

> Venimos, por tanto, a luchar porque el país se constituya. Obra lenta y enorme que formará el objeto de nuestras labores en la política fundamental.[49]

The constitutional principles and the legal precepts should become reality. Sánchez Santos advocated the rule of law, not men; in this he was consistent if not necessarily realistic.

For him, México was yet to be constituted into a State. It could become so, however, through a firm, moral religious base, ethnic unity, education and propitious laws and government. Currently the spirit and the letter of the law did not determine the functioning of government authority, a fault which, in turn, was related to the lack of a moral base. The State and its laws ought to protect and advance social Christian interests.[50] He firmly endorsed democracy as the form of government and felt that Catholic religious beliefs would strengthen its practice, though he allowed that for the Church there was no *one* form of government; it solely asked of government the liberty to function.

Over the years he was a consistent, though not a violence-prone, critic of the regime. Sánchez Santos viewed Díaz as politically able and administratively capable; but in the social sphere his regime was a disaster, and as early as 1903 Sánchez Santos warned that serious consequences were bound to follow its social policies or lack of them.[51] Sánchez Santos was a severe critic and exposer of caciquismo, and was relentlessly courageous in his attack. From caciquismo flowed national disunity, corruption and injustice, and these factors were to be found at national, state, and local levels. In addition to caciquismo, the denial of democracy and freedom of the press were his most vigorous complaints against the Díaz regime. Sánchez Santos advocated that criticism of the government was, for the journalist, the preeminent patriotic obligation.[52]

In retrospect, a critical turn in the thought and advocation of Sánchez Santos occurred in the mid-1890s. This was associated with the crisis of Western society of which he was hyperconscious, the developing crisis in México, and the publication and influence of Leo XIII's encyclical *Rerum Novarum* (1891):

> Todo el magisterio de León XIII se dirige en el fondo a la solución de nuestros *problemas sociales* [his italics]; mas aquel en que da forma sintética a todas esas grandiosas enseñanzas, aquel en que sale a atacar al monstruo de frente, aquel en que se plantea en concreta, el problema y en concreto se resuelve, ese monumento de justicia de sabidura y de ternura, se llama: la enciclica "*Rerum Novarum.*"[53]

The encyclical helped to clarify Sánchez Santos' thought by providing a cohesive view and position premised on values and beliefs he already accepted, thus giving him a new impetus for his advocacy. The encyclical dealt with the questions of the eternal happiness of man, the well-being of society and the urgency of el problema social in a time of crisis. Social justice was the solution of the crisis and it was imperative that Christians act. The base of true reform was the restoration of Christian values as well as equality and justice for men. These would bring about national salvation and greatness. The State, through the participation of Christians, was to be an aid in this process. As Sánchez Santos interpreted the encyclical, the virtues of charity and sacrifice in behalf of others were indispensable for the salvation of man and the building of a great and just fatherland.[54] These were the antidotes for the negative and selfish values that had brought on the crisis, a crisis which was at the root of the conflict between capital and labor and which threatened the Western world and México. As a result, people were rising against authority and property, an uprising which would end with the destruction of religion and the State—a possibility Sánchez Santos would not tolerate. Anarchism and atheism were intertwined; the forces of Christianity must be arrayed against them, and to succeed, the rights of capital and labor had to be synthesized.

Sánchez Santos argued that there was a "natural right" to property and a corresponding obligation to distribute wealth.[55] The distinction was between the thing and its products: the first could be undeniably private, the second had a social and public character and called for equitable distribution in order to provide for the spiritual-social well-being of all. Wealth ought to be distributed for the good of the wealthy and others. The State can be active in this process; it must be just and have internal integrity, that is, observe and protect civil rights and responsibilities. Sánchez Santos saw education as having two aspects: imparting knowledge which involved enlarging the educational system, and the moral-spiritual, or to him, the ideological content of education. Naturally he admitted that the latter was more important to him than the former. What was important to him was the purpose of education, that being the promotion of the general public welfare.

In a series of presentations before the Pedagogical Congress of 1897, he made a display of his considerable rhetorical and polemical talents. The argument he presented held that since the purpose of education was the public good and since religion was indeed the best vehicle for accomplishing it, religion ought to be allowed to be taught in the schools to those whose parents desired it.[56] He believed that secularizing education meant depriving it of its Catholic content and since for him Catholicism and patriotism were integral, he saw the separation of religion from the curriculum as favoring the "masonic-protestant" aim of weakening México.

He was among the publicists who helped convince the society of the importance and urgency of education. He believed it was a means for national progress indispensable in the modern age. The problem of rural education and of schools for the Indians was emphasized constantly in his writings. He was a critic of the regime because it did not consider rural educational needs, especially those of the Indian.

He believed the colonial missionary effort was the model for contemporary work among the Indian. From his earliest period Sánchez Santos was one of the writers most noticeably concerned with the Indian.[57] He advocated a spiritual, educational and economic mission to the Indian:

> Apresurémonos, señores, a colaborar en esa gran obra . . . la obra de crear una nación, y una *gran nación* [his italics], que substituya a este hacinamiento de gentes colecticias, expuesto a ser presa de cualquier vecino codicioso.
> Acudamos con el amor inmenso de la patria.[58]

He was even more insistent over the injustice to the Indian than he was with other social sectors for which he expressed concern. He identified the problem as economic:

> Yo creo que el problema indigena descansa ante todo, en factores económicos.[59]

The Indian's standard of living had to be raised before anything else, including spiritual welfare and education. He felt that the work had to be done in a spirit of charity and love or the Indian would not be reached. Unrealistically, he considered the Church capable of such work, but significantly he demanded State action as well.

Like many others of his time, he felt, rather than understood, the agrarian problem; like nearly everyone else except the peasants, he was oblivious to the desire for land. But he did perceive the problem early and proceeded from a purely moral judgment to specific reforms. He saw it within a larger perspective:

> El Problema Nacional Mexicano, problema de vida, está constítuido por dos extremos terribles: en la periferia, la civilización fascinadora, la riqueza aplastante, el poderío supremo de los Estados Unidos de América; en el centro, las tres grandes misérias de las

tres cuartas partes de la población mejicana, la población agrícola: la miséria moral, la miséria ecónomica y la miséria fisiológica.[60]

As Sánchez Santos saw it in 1904, the rural problem fitted within the context of the larger national problem which had two aspects, the internal and the external. The latter involved the United States, its sheer physical presence, in addition to its economic, political, and military preeminence. Explicitly anti-American he tenaciously fought American influence in México in every area. He saw the United States as a threat to national sovereignty, unity, and progress. The possibility for felicitous handling of the external problem presented by the United States depended on the solution to the internal situation:

> Grandes, muy grandes fueron los que lograron nuestra emancipación política; mas el verdadero "Gloria en excelsis" de la historia moderna mexicana será para los que conquistan nuestra emancipación económica.
>
> Entonces resonarán con el acento puro de la verdad, estas dos palabras tan deliciosas para nosotros: *México libre* [his italics].[61]

The major internal domestic liability for progress, he analyzed, was the rural condition in humane and ecological terms which, in effect, meant three-quarters of México. The situation was one of dismal physiological, economic and moral poverty. The solutions proposed by him were, in general: to upgrade the quality of life and the quantity of production; uplift the campesino with a system of rural education and provide him with a moral invigorization; and end the alcoholism and high mortality rate. Sánchez Santos felt that first, production must be increased by irrigation and fertilization which would, in turn, raise the standard of living by providing higher salaries. Thus for Sánchez Santos this was no longer merely a problem of Christianization, but one of material reforms. By the end of his life he was more specific, going so far as to request State solutions.

Sánchez Santos developed increasing concern for the condition of urban labor after 1900, one which at first he saw as separate from the problems of rural labor. Not unexpectedly, he approached it first as a problem of morality. In this he was with the majority opinion of the times. He saw poverty as a result of vice. The condition of the laboring classes was a result of the prevalence of prostitutes, thievery, and alcoholism. Sánchez

Santos denounced these social ills. The solution was the Christianization of the working poor which would alter their moral and economic situation. Originally he implicitly saw the organizing of workers in mutualista associations (self help worker groups) as irrelevant, for the issue, as stated previously, was one of morality. Furthermore, these organizations were anti-Christian, an accusation he did not explain.

By the mid-1890s he was moving away from this position. Labor, he believed, must be incorporated into the national society for the sake of justice and national stability.[62] The workers had a right to a just wage which adequately met their needs and provided a fair standard of living. This, he felt, was a Christian imperative. Furthermore, he viewed the laborer as the single most important element in the national society, and by 1909 he believed that it was now, like it or not, the determining class. In 1910, with the full force of the now very influential *El País*, he demanded a minimum salary for all workers, acknowledging that this would entail an intricate equitable national scheme and that the State, if there were no other remedy, could intervene in behalf of labor, though preferably not:

> El salario mínimo pertenece a la justicia estricta. Así es que el Estado podría en tesis hacer respetar la justicia, en esta como en otra materia.[63]

Though he had previously been hostile to the tactic, he called for the support of the strike as a weapon, and organization of unions and cooperatives as the vehicles for obtaining wage increases.

What made him a critic of the Díaz regime was to make him a critic of the Madero experiment, though perhaps not with as much justification or understanding. Sánchez Santos endorsed and advocated the need for a democratic-reform opposition movement.[64] Yet in his judgment Madero should not have been the candidate because he lacked the prestige and the experience for a national political leader; he would not be able to manage or hold together the movement. Yet Sánchez Santos respected Madero's integrity and intentions and reluctantly supported him in the 1910 and 1911 campaigns. He identified two elements in the opposition to the regime: the well-intentioned, disinterested idealists and those who were self-interested opportunists.[65] The latter were no different and would be no different from those in office, except that they were "out" and wanted "in."[66] Nonetheless, Sánchez Santos supported the Revolution because it encompassed national ideals and popular aspirations.[67]

Sánchez Santos rejected the wanton violence and destruction that resulted from the Madero revolt and believed that it had unleashed emotions and energies that could only have long-term grievous consequences. His disillusionment with the revolution was, as he pointed out, due to four reasons: 1. the depredations of the Zapatistas; 2. the imposition of candidates and officeholders at the national, state, and local level, which he felt to be a continuation of practices under Díaz; 3. the continuing influence of ex-porfiristas and científicos; and 4. the continuing electoral fraud.[68] His criticism of the new regime became increasingly bitter toward the time of his death. Nonetheless, he advocated support of the Madero government as a patriotic obligation and the only recourse in the face of anarchy and disintegration.[69] The new government was failing because men were not worthy of their historical moment.

As a whole, Sánchez Santos worked out a synthesis for the furtherance and strengthening of the fatherland and religion, one which joined the responsibilities of both a patriot and a Catholic in being a defender of both tradition and progress. He, like Sierra, championed and furthered nationalism. His motivation stemmed from his anxiety for the spiritual and material greatness of the patria. He contributed especially in the area of socioeconomic political criticism extending patriotism to include justice for all citizens in this area. He certainly was religiously, socially, and economically xenophobic. His sense of nation was inclusive of all sectors of society. He contributed to the development of a nationalist climate as a gifted writer and moving speaker and, importantly, through his newspaper which had a large audience. Ricardo Flores Magón also had an audience and he too shared the concern for México, but from a different perspective.

## RICARDO FLORES MAGÓN

Ricardo Flores Magón is as perplexing as he is important. Often dismissed as an illusionary, impractical thinker, he was very much a reflection of his age and certainly a major contributor to the intellectual climate and political process of the time.[70] Though his life went beyond the limits of this study, his early years and those of his maturity and greatest influence in México coincide within the framework of 1890-1911. He was the most radical spokesman of the day and his influence was important in transcending nineteenth century liberalism.

Ricardo Flores Magón came of age in the *Porfiriato*, influenced by the education then in vogue, and reflecting the anxieties of his generation. He was also the bearer of the Mexican Liberal inheritance of the nineteenth century. He was closer to the "puro" rather than the "moderado" variety of liberals. His thought evolved over time; yet there are certain constants as well as changes and contradictions in his ideas.

The education that he received in his youth was to strongly mark his writings and political tactics. He received a positivist education that stressed rational analysis and objectivity. This educational framework upheld the primacy of the material world which, according to positivism, followed "laws." It viewed the world as evolving, and viewed all spheres of life as relative. Life, as struggle, was an integral premise in this world view but so was a utilitarianism that held good for the greater number, the efficacy of personal volition, and the ideal of personal liberty. Man had the potential for improvement through effort and education; moral and material progress was both possible and real.

Flores Magón, as he received these particular analytical tools and premises for approaching and dealing with the world, also turned to other influences that provided a political and social complement. Throughout his life he read classical literature such as Shakespeare and the naturalist writers.[71] From childhood, because of his family, he was inclined to liberalism as a political creed. Through his writings during the years 1900-1911, he showed a thorough knowledge of the Juárez generation. Up to his conversion to anarchism, he upheld the Constitution of 1857 as an ideal.

Flores Magón amended and rejected some of these formative influences during his lifetime. He maintained throughout, however, a critical view of life, remained a materialist, and firmly pegged his political ideas to conform to a world of natural laws. Life was worth living for him and what disorder there was, he felt man could bring to harmony through rational reasoning. Yet in his thought there was always theoretical and humanist preoccupations. He held as goals for political activity solidarity, generosity, selflessness, harmony, and material well-being. He later questioned progress through evolution; the solution was revolution to reestablish progress. He became convinced that the problems of México were integrally associated with worldwide factors. This realization affected his focus of concern. To change México, the world had to be changed—thus he became an internationalist.

    Flores Magón and his two brothers, Jesús and Enrique, shared, in their youth at least, the same liberal ideals and a strong mutual attachment. Through 1902 they were to function as a group; in fact, his brothers were Flores Magón's first political cadre. Jesús broke away in 1903 but Enrique remained with Ricardo up until the time Ricardo died. Ricardo Flores Magón emerged in politics as a student leader in anti-Porfirista demonstrations carried out by students in la ciudad de México in 1892, though he was not the principal student spokesman.[72] Sixty students and others protested for free elections and against the continuance of Díaz in office. As a result, Flores Magón received his first jail sentence. In 1893, along with other students, he established *El Demócrata*, a Liberal opposition newspaper which was suppressed within a year. Little is known of his life from the period of his dissociation from this paper to the time when *Regeneración* appears in 1900.[73]

    With Jesús Flores Magón, Antonio Horcasitas, and himself as the senior editors, Ricardo Flores Magón established *Regeneración* as a "periodico juridico independiente." The first issue appeared on August 7, 1900.[74] The name refers to the regeneration of the patria. At this time *Regeneración* was reformist and limited to legal and juridical concerns, reflecting the professional interests and youthful ideals of the editors. Jesús and Horcasitas were lawyers and Ricardo was a law student. The first nineteen issues of *Regeneración*, up to December 23, 1900, dealt with problems in the administration of justice in la ciudad de México and the provinces. It stated judicial grievances by highlighting specific cases of judicial corruption.[75] Flores Magón did not banter rhetoric. Already cognizant that patriotism was a rationale used by the regime to claim allegiance from the people and to instill militarism, he argued for a patriotism that was based on civic virtues and stressed harmony.[76] However, he did see patriotism as a prime motivation and justification for his own actions and exhortations. In a letter written in 1905, he said:

sobre todo y sobre todos, *está la salvación* de la patria.[77]

He did not take up directly the role of the State; by implication its function was good government, which could be accomplished by adhering to the Constitution and wielding only those powers specifically granted to it. The United States he saw as a potential threat because it might absorb México.[78] Foreign economic predominance was not specifically questioned; in fact, commentary on foreign events was strangely absent; neither land nor economic grievances were taken up directly, although he clearly gave material well-being increasing importance. Also, at this time his writings lacked attention to the problema indígena.

On December 31, 1900, *Regeneración* declared itself, "un periodico independiente de combate;" Horcasitas dropped out from the editorial board and only the three brothers continued.[79] It was still a reformist newspaper, but one that was frankly political, and in opposition to the regime.

The view of the national past, and later that of the world at large, as well as the judgment of the contemporary state of society, was central to Flores Magón's thinking. He shared the general liberal view of his generation on history and contemporary society, though becoming increasingly pessimistic and apocalyptic. He saw Mexican history as one of continuous struggle for the freedom and well-being of the people and as one of repression and suffering:

> habiendo luchado todo el siglo XIX, estamos condenados a seguir luchando por ella en el presente.[80]

He dated this national struggle from the Conquest to the present, identifying it with the struggle of the Aztecs against the Spaniards and continuing through the Colonial period and through the nineteenth century to his time. For him the oppressors were the Spaniards, the Church, the landowners, and the military. This view of history was nationalistic, the people were the nation, their oppressors were the national enemies, the people's victories the national victories. Later, the traditional oppressive sectors were to be joined by foreigners—the French and the Anglo. He saw the Reforma as the one glimmer of freedom and democracy in Mexican history but the Díaz dictatorship ended the era. Hence the Mexicans, he concluded, were historically condemned to struggle until free. Flores Magón issued a call for continuance, though there was a certain melancholia in his advocation. In this view the only heroes were the people and, perhaps, the leadership of the Reform.

In Flores Magón's analysis, the causes of this negative situation were the clergy, the military, and bad government, abetted by the innocence of a gullible people.[81] Yet during his early period, Flores Magón, like others of his generation, readily saw progress, both material and moral. However, he eventually arrived at the conclusion that without material well-being there cannot be progress in other spheres. In his early period he placed faith in personal will and education as a means of correcting the negative national situation. He principally indicted the indifference of the people, their estrangement from politics, and their failure to struggle. He insisted these facts could change—a change made possible by informing, encouraging, and educating the people.

Flores Magón was clearly in the mainstream of Mexican Liberalism and remained a strong publicist for it until 1906. His personal motivation was the love and well-being of the nation which to him was composed of the middle class, the workers (urban and rural) and the Indians.[82] He advocated fidelity to democratic practices and a reinstatement of the Constitution of 1857:

> Lucharemos sin discanso hasta el logro de nuestros ideales, pensando siempre que esos mismos ideales fueron los de nuestros padres del 57, sustenidos vigorosamente en la tribuna, en el libro, en la prensa y en los campos de batalla.[83]

His opinion and depiction of the general citizenry was ambivalent. He upheld them as sovereign and heroic yet also viewed the people as submissive:

> El pueblo, que es el soberano o más bien dicho, entre nosotros debiera ser el soberano puesto que las autoridades en toda democracia emanan el pueblo, que es el único que puede nombrarlas, ese mismo pueblo ayer fuerte y viril, ahora se ve sometido por sus mismos servidores.[84]

To correct this, there were men of good-will and sound principles who could provide direction and organization. He believed that political organizing and reform were possible and positive even under the Díaz regime. For Flores Magón at this stage, 1900–1906, the political situation called for the reorganization of the Liberal Party and the coalescing of it around a deserving independent candidate, unassociated with the regime. When the Liberal Party began to form in 1900 he was a strong supporter. In his early period he rejected revolution as counter-productive to progress and advocated civic responsibility and political organization.[85] Later, Flores Magón was to reject all politics as futile, except those of violence.

In 1900 the Flores Magón brothers joined the call for the formation of liberal clubs; Ricardo became a major spokesman and leader of the Congress at San Luís Potosí in February, 1901. Flores Magón exerted a major influence at this historic affair and by April, with Diodoro Batalla and others, formed *La Associación Liberal Reformista*, a liberal club in Mexico City associated with the Congress.[86] He was becoming not only a writer and spokesman, but also an organizer. Since he was now questioning the legitimacy of the regime, not only writing and speaking but also taking part in organizing opposition, he was a marked man. From 1901 through 1903 he was fined and sentenced three times and eventually prohibited from writing in México.[87] *Regeneración* was suppressed as were *El Hijo del Ahuizote* and several other newspapers which he attempted to start or with which he collaborated. The choice for him was to continue to be sent to prison or complete inactivity; rather than do either he chose exile in the United States on January 3, 1904.[88]

Flores Magón, during 1900 to 1906, had passed from moral criticism to one that was political; eventually he was to adopt one that was ethical, social, and economic as well. In effect, he underwent an evolution in his thinking—one that radicalized and expanded his intellectual horizons. It was a process visible among liberals and the public, though not as acute. Criticism of one sphere of political life, the judiciary, eventually raised questions about political administration as a whole.

Flores Magón and his adherents were among the first to question and to convince others to question the legitimacy as well as the political viability of the regime.[89] A beneficent dictatorship did not provide the basis for social, economic, or political development necessary for national progress; in fact, it was counter-productive even for the economy. All sectors suffered, including the bourgeoisie, thus all had a common cause. Harmony was a possibility and a necessity; progressive politics could be based on this. He also pointed out that liberals ought to go beyond a dated, irrelevant, anti-clericalism and take a harder realistic look at causes for national ills.[90] Flores Magón argued and demonstrated that the citizenry could be aroused, educated to the issues and organized; and he stressed that what was needed was for *good men*, truly patriotic, to unite in a political force and to struggle:

Hagamos saber nuestra voluntad, que es la voluntad nacional.[91]

This required a love of democracy, some good faith, and dedication to the national welfare.[92] Not surprising the *Plan* of 1906, emanating from Flores Magón and his associates, was the first coherent statement on needed universal reforms which transcended nineteenth century liberalism and clearly pointed into the twentieth century. From the perspective of Flores Magón's personal evolution and public influence, the 1906 statement was a summation and watershed. It was postulated on the potential harmony of all national sectors within a reformed state.

The next stage in his development was to be constant with former ideals as a result of self-criticism of past ideas. His development was influenced also by his failures in direct organizing. To this assimilation of experience and self-criticism were added a new influence and environment. Anarchism was in vogue and available; it provided a coherent, tactical and ideological perspective; it stressed accepted ideals. Flores Magón in 1901 had said:

La idea liberal es la de la libertad.[93]

Anarchism often appeared in agrarian traditional societies of the nineteenth century undergoing modern transformation and strain.[94]

The new phase was to require clandestine organizing and armed rebellion. Flores Magón broke with such as Camilo Arriaga and Madero in 1906 though the public rapture with the latter did not materialize until 1911.[95] From 1906 through 1911, his influence was significant because of his organizing activity, his writings, and because he had, for a while, the rudimentary framework of a political group and national prestige.

In a letter dated 1908 to two of his closest adherents, Flores Magón sent new analyses and tactics.[96] In his view, the history of revolutions in México and elsewhere demonstrated that they were cyclical and futile. At great sacrifice, and with good intentions, power was taken, yet tyranny eventually resulted. The legislative process, participated in by all classes and including all political views, gradually lost impetus and became conservative as it attempted institutionalization. The people continued in poverty and without political liberty; this because the root causes—private property and the values surrounding it—remained. As long as this was so, exploitation and suppression would result. Private property had to be abolished and a process of permanent revolution had to be engineered.

Flores Magón outlined in the letter that the strategy should be to initiate the revolution, and to insure that pent-up frustrations and desires were given free reign. He envisioned that a Mexican revolution would have strong anticapitalist tendencies. He advised giving the land away and letting the people take over the mines and factories; first the national bourgeoisie would be disposed of, foreign owners later. In the process the people would learn solidarity and mutual cooperation; relations should be established with socialist and anarchist organizations in other countries. Flores Magón counted on a minority of dedicated, principled individuals and on support from anarchists and socialists for the work that this plan entailed. Because of the connotations of the term anarchism, he cautioned that for tactical reasons it should not be used publicly. Such were the views he held for the following period, 1908–1911.

The first issue of *Regeneración*, published in Los Angeles (September 3, 1910), aimed at rallying the Mexican people.[97] It called for violent revolution, denounced foreign capital, and advocated the sovereignty of the people as transcendent over office-holders and institutions. Political liberty, it argued, requires economic liberty and equality to be effective:

La libertad política requiere la concurrencia de otra libertad para ser effectiva; esa libertad es la económica.[98]

It pointed out that workers produce the wealth, thus it should be theirs. He no longer saw harmony but rather class conflict. At the same time he stressed the equality of women and the need for their freedom as integral to true social liberation.[99]

In various issues of his newspapers, he advocated a more radical perspective. Directing himself to orthodox Liberalism, he argued that equality was the base for fraternity and liberty, yet the three traditional liberal goals were impossible while social classes, acquisitiveness and competition existed. Electoral democracy always was controlled by the wealthy against everyone else.[100] Since land was the basic form of wealth in México, it must be distributed equally and immediately; that should be the first objective.[101] The cry was land and liberty.

Admittedly, foreign capital was seen as a major exploiter of the people and supporter of tyranny. However, he denounced hatred between nationalities which impeded universal brotherhood and was a result of capitalism.

Flores Magón foresaw and urged revolution. He presented an analysis of its likely development. In a moving plea, he postulated two alternatives for the revolution: merely political reform, or a thorough social and economic transformation. To Flores Magón none of the historical movements of the Mexican people had resulted in progress, regardless of free elections or sincere candidates. He counseled that the Mexican poor must fight for their class interests against the despot Díaz, and anyone else.[102] A bourgeois republic was unsatisfactory for the real needs of the people.[103] Because it comes back after a period of harsh repression that affected all sectors, the Revolution would set loose deep popular discontent, the true revolutionary force. The Revolution, however, would have contradictory elements, hence the working sectors must be wary of reform bourgeoisie leadership capturing it for their own class interests.

Accordingly, he took pains to point out the differences between his "El Partido Liberal Mexicano" and Madero's "Partido anti-reeleccionista."[104] He announced that the Partido Liberal was interested in the distribution of land and the means of production with the goals of fraternity, equality, and freedom as the proper national, social, and economic ideals.[105] He said that the utopia he advocated was possible; there was the historical precedent of the Mexican Indian communities.

By 1911 he was moving away from overt patriotism, though his appeals were Mexican and he never rejected love of culture or region. He rationalized that these were encompassed in the greater patria, la tierra.[106]

By 1912 his influence was declining. Perhaps this was due to his living out of the country or his increasingly utopian goals. In 1922 death rescued him from near oblivion. The pattern of his thought and action was subject to reasoned objectivity, emotional intuition, logic, and irrationality. His driving impetus was his concern for the welfare of the citizens:

> ese amor sacrosanto de la patria es, y ha sido, el movil de todos nuestros actos.[107]

Flores Magón was important for the development of nationalism for several reasons. He was a major influence in politically radicalizing the Mexican people during the years 1900–1911. His contributions to the nationalist process were political ideals and organizational activity. He stressed that sovereignty resided in the people and that there was nothing above it. In the early years before 1908 he publicized that government, i.e., the State, must reflect the will of the people or it was illegitimate. His sense of national community was all inclusive. Anarchism was an extension of the horizons of his concern, not a lessening of his concern for México and things Mexican. His nationalism came to mean the advocation of revolution. Manuel González Ramírez has rightfully hailed Flores Magón as "ideólogo del nacionalismo mexicano."[108] Gonzalo Aquirre Beltran has singled out his major historical importance:

> Con Marx, Bakunin, Blanqui, Mazzini y otros rebeldes paso a formar parte de ese grupo singular de precursores de las grandes revoluciones de nuestra epoca.[109]

Sierra, Sánchez Santos and Flores Magón clarified traditional values and views. They also introduced relatively new values and perspectives to a large audience, and individually reflected the effects of social change.

NOTES

1. John Friedman, "Intellectuals in Developing Societies," *Kyklos* (1960), pp. 513–544.
2. Ibid., pg. 521.
3. For a biography of Sierra see Agustín Yañez, *Don Justo Sierra* (México, D.F.: Universidad Nacional Autónoma de México, 1962), *passim*. Sierra's collected works contain much biographical data. Sources for his ideas are found in Justo Sierra, *Obras completas del Maestro Justo Sierra*, Vols. 1–14, Agustín Yañez, ed., (México, D.F.: Universidad Nacional Autónoma de México, 1948).
4. Justo Sierra, *Obras completas*, Vol. 7.
5. The first group adamantly advocated a strict adherence to the Constitution of 1857; the second supported a strict social dictatorship; the third desired generally a monarchy or a return to the Constitution of 1836 and close Church-State relations.
6. Justo Sierra, *Obras completas*, Vol. 4, pp. 157–167; see also Vol. 5, pp. 101–115, Vol. 9, pp. 58–79, and Vol. 4, pp. 81–83.
7. Ibid., Vol. 8, pg. 98.
8. Ibid., Vol. 4, pp. 123–125.
9. Ibid., Vol. 4, pg. 134.
10. Ibid., Vol. 12, pg. 362.
11. Ibid., Vol. 5, pp. 101–115.

12. Compare the writings in Vol. 4, pp. 172-290, to the *Manifiesto de la Convención Liberal* (1892) in Manuel González Ramírez, ed., *Fuentes para la historia de la revolución Mexicana*, Vol. IV, *Manifiestos Políticos*, 4 vols., (México, D.F.: Fondo de Cultura Económica, 1954), pp. 3-13.

13. Ibid., Vol. 5, pg. 411.
14. Ibid., Vol. 4, pg. 125.
15. Ibid., Vol. 5, pg. 414.
16. During his life, Sierra took a number of trips abroad that influenced him. The first, in 1895, to the United States, made his attitude toward the country more apprehensive and ambivalent; whereas before, he had been an admirer, as can be seen in his book, *En Tierra Yankee*. A trip to Europe, 1900-1901, had a similar cooling effect on his attitude to that general area, but his appreciation and empathy for Spain deepened. Travel strengthened his belief that México must seek its own way (Ibid., Vol. 6, *passim*). He was elected President at the Hispanic-American Congress at Madrid in 1900. He argued in his address for obligatory rather than voluntary arbitration; for making the Monroe Doctrine a Pan-American policy; for Latin Unity (through rejecting the notion of "Latin race"), and for national self-determination (Ibid., Vol. 5, pg. 277).

17. Ibid., Vol. 5, pg. 139; Ibid., Vol. 12, pg. 220. As his general perspective, Sierra held that history was the scientific, documented, record of the development of the human species and its efforts to dominate nature. When he said "scientific" he meant based on ascertained facts, the synthesizing of these and the presentation of rigorous rational analysis. In this process there was no place for emotion. In accordance with his views on society, history was organic; the past, the present, man and nature, were organically connected. However, this was not simply material but ideal. It was the revelation of the "ser-en-sí" of humanity, the transcendence over nature and ideals. History was the continuing effort to realize absolute values. To understand this nonmaterial aspect of history, the historian well-versed in scientific methodology must also use intuition and be a poet to convey his insight.

18. Ibid., Vol. 12, pg. 361.
19. Ibid., Vol. 14, pg. 100.
20. Ibid., Vol. 12, pp. 178-288.
21. Ibid., Vol. 12, pg. 220.
22. Ibid., Vol. 8, pp. 60-64.
23. Ibid., Vol. 12, pg. 395.
24. Ibid., Vol. 8, pg. 13.
25. Ibid., Vol. 4, pg. 221.
26. Ibid., Vol. 8, pp. 34-41.
27. Ibid., Vol. 13, pp. 537.
28. Ibid., Vol. 8, pp. 221-222.
29. Ibid., pg. 252.
30. Ibid.
31. Ibid., pp. 255-256.
32. Ibid., pp. 259-261.
33. Ibid., pg. 56.
34. Ibid., pg. 19.
35. Ibid., pp. 328-329.
36. Ibid., Vol. 5, pg. 431.
37. Ibid., pg. 323.

38. Ibid., pg. 437.
39. Ibid., Vol. 9, pg. 291; Vol. 5, pp. 441-442; Vol. 14, pg. 64.
40. The motto for his newspaper, *El País*, 1899-1912.
41. Consult Trinidad Sánchez Santos, *Obras selectas de Don Trinidad Sánchez* (2 vols.; Dr. Octaviano Márquez, ed.; México, D.F.: Editorial Jus. 1962). Biographical information may be culled from the introductory note by Dr. Márquez (the late archbishop of Puebla) in these volumes, pp. 7-31, and in the introduction by Luís Íslas García, ed., *Trinidad Sánchez Santos* (México, D.F.: Editorial Jus., 1946), pp. 11-108.
42. Luís Íslas García, ed., *Trinidad Sánchez Santos* (México, D.F.: Editorial Jus. 1945), pp. 89-90.
43. *Obras*, Vol. I, pg. 177.
44. *El País*, passim; Sánchez Santos, *Obras*, Vol. II, pp. 46-47.
45. *Obras*, Vol. II, pp. 269-271.
46. Ibid., Vol. I, pp. 276-299.
47. Ibid., Vol. II, pg. 259.
48. Ibid., Vol. I, pp. 270-275.
49. Ibid., Vol. II, pp. 318-319.
50. Ibid., pp. 103-104.
51. Sánchez Santos, *El País*, January 1, 1903.
52. *Obras*, Vol. II, pp. 315-316.
53. *Obras*, Vol. I, pg. 99.
54. Ibid., pp. 81-111.
55. Ibid., pp. 104-106.
56. Ibid., pp. 176-193.
57. Ibid., pp. 276-299.
58. Ibid., pg. 274.
59. Ibid., pg. 288.
60. Ibid., pg. 147.
61. Ibid., pp. 147-148.
62. Trinidad Sánchez Santos, *Editoriales de El País*, Manuel Leon Sánchez, ed., (México, D.F.: Ediciones León Sánchez, 1923), pp. 47-52.
63. Ibid., pg. 48.
64. Ibid., pg. 17.
65. Sánchez Santos, *Obras*, Vol. 2, pg. 383.
66. Sánchez Santos, *Editoriales*, pp. 35-42.
67. *El País*, May 26, 1911.
68. Sánchez Santos, *Editoriales*, pp. 277-282.
69. Sánchez Santos, *Obras*, Vol. 2, pg. 55.
70. For biographical information see Ethel Duffy Turner, *Ricardo Flores Magón y el Partido Liberal Mexicano*, trans. Eduardo Limón G. Morelia (Michoacán: Editorial Erandi, 1960).
71. Consult Eduardo Blanquel, *El pensamiento Político de Ricardo Flores Magón* (México, D.F.: Universidad Nacional Autónoma de México, Facultad de Filosofía y Letras, 1963).
72. Letter from Ricardo Florẹs Magón to Gus Teltch, Aptil 28, 1921 in José Muñoz Cota, *Ricardo Flores Magón, El sueño de una palabra* (México, D.F.: Editorial Doctrimex, 1966), pg. 48.
73. Samuel Kaplan in *Peleamos Contra la Injusticia* (México, D.F.: Libro-Mex, 1960), reports that Enrique Flores Magón stated that the brothers attended

law school, worked in law offices, and saved their money for the establishment of a newspaper. See pp. 57-60.
74. *Regeneración*, August 7, 1900.
75. Ibid., August 7-December 23, 1900.
76. Ibid., August 15, 1901.
77. Letter to Francisco M. Ibarra, December 28, 1905, reproduced in Manuel González Ramírez, ed., *Fuentes para la historia de la revolución mexicana*, Vol. 3, *La huelga de Cananea*, pg. 7.
78. *Regeneración*, April 23, 1901.
79. Ibid., August 7, 1900.
80. Ibid., January 7, 1901.
81. Ibid., August 7, 1901.
82. Ibid., June 23, 1901.
83. Ibid., December 31, 1900.
84. Ibid., November 23, 1900.
85. Ibid., April 15, 1901.
86. Turner, *Ricardo Flores Magón y el Partido Liberal Mexicano*, pp. 35-36.
87. Diego Abad de Santillán, *Ricardo Flores Magón* (México D.F.: Grupo Cultural "Ricardo Flores Magón," 1925), pp. 7-12.
88. Turner, pg. 65.
89. Ibid., August 7, 1901.
90. Ibid., March 31, 1901.
91. Ibid., March 7, 1901.
92. Ibid., March 7, 1901.
93. Ibid., August 15, 1901.
94. Consult George Woodcock, *Anarchism, A History of Libertarian Ideas and Movements* (Cleveland and New York: The World Publishing Company, 1962), *passim*.
95. Letter to Antonio de P. Araugo, June 6, 1907, in *Epistolario*, pp. 107-110.
96. Letter to Praxedio Guerrero and Enrique Flores Magón, June 13, 1908, in *Epistolario*, pp. 202-209.
97. *Regeneración*, September 3, 1910.
98. Ibid.
99. Ibid., September 24, 1910.
100. Ibid., October 8, 1910.
101. Ibid., October 1, 1910.
102. Ibid., May 23, 1911.
103. Ibid., February 11, 1911.
104. Ibid., November 5, 1910.
105. Ibid., April 3, 1911.
106. Ibid., January 27, 1912.
107. Ibid., May 16, 1910.
108. Manuel González Ramírez, *Epistolario y textos*, pg. 17.
109. Gonzalo Aguirre Beltran, ed., *Ricardo Flores Magón, Antología* (México, D.F.: Universidad Nacional Autónoma de México, 1970), pg. x.

# George Sánchez and Testing

**RICHARD E. LÓPEZ**
**JULIAN SAMORA**

The major issues surrounding the mental testing of subordinate groups in the 1970s include the heredity-versus-environment controversy, the effect of bilingualism on test performance, and the validity of tests.[1] George Sánchez tackled all these issues in the early 1930s in an effort to insure equal educational opportunities for the Spanish-speaking.

George Sánchez recognized heredity as a legitimate avenue of investigation in the pursuit of explanations which account for intergroup differences on mental tests; however, he felt many investigators did not give careful consideration to environmental or linguistic explanations. He stated that the interpretation of test results should not fail to consider important differences in personal, social, and cultural histories and milieu. He recognized that bilingual children had special problems in Anglo-oriented schools which include the inability to use the school language efficiently[2] and possibly an environmentally based confusion hindering the expression of innate ability.[3]

In one instance, an investigator accepted the hereditary explanation (i.e. the lower scores represent low inate ability) assuming that language handicaps should disappear as a result of schooling,[4] hence there should be increases in mental test scores in each succeeding grade. Dr. Sánchez pointed out that even if the language handicap was reduced substantially with progress in grades, the handicap could still exist and might be even greater because of the progressively greater amounts of language required in succeeding grades.

Some people in the 1970s accept the idea that heredity contributes more than environment in the determination of intelligence.[5] Kagan (1971) outlined and evaluated some of the major reasons for this acceptance. Like George Sánchez, he doubted the heredity arguments[6] because IQ tests are culturally biased instruments. Kagan also doubted the genetic argument because ". . . similar IQ scores of genetically related people can be simulated in genetically unrelated people who live in similar environments . . ." and ". . . the probable correlation between heredity and environment is ignored in current interpretations of the heritability ratio." Sánchez also criticized those accepting environmental explanations:

> On the environmental side we find little scientific analysis of the influence of environment on test results. Usually investigators have been content to make a rough estimate of living conditions of the subjects under consideration and then to suggest a possible relationship between low socioeconomic status and the low scores on the test.

Mercer (1972) accepted this challenge and developed a sociocultural index for classifying children by family background. Using seventeen background variables and the full WISC (Wechsler Intelligence Scale for Children) IQ, a series of stepwise multiple regressions yielded five primary background variables (those most strongly related to IQ).[7] The sample consisted of 598 Chicano children (ages 6-14) representing the total Chicano student population of three segregated minority elementary schools in Riverside, California. Children were assigned scores from 0-5 depending on how many of these background characteristics the child's family shared with the typical Anglo family in Riverside. The results showed that Chicano children as a group had an average IQ below the national norm; however, when the Chicano child's family shared all five background characteristics with the typical Anglo family the average IQ was considerably above the national norm (104.4 and 99.5 respectively).

George Sánchez believed that the study of the effect of language problems on bilingual children's performance on mental tests was handicapped by difficulties in measurement. Translated tests were of doubtful value because of questionable equivalence to originals and could be questioned further on the basis of cultural content. Literature reviews of recent studies suggest the measurement problem is still with us. These reviews show contradictory results across a number of studies and sometimes unwarranted conclusions are made (Sattler, 1972; Zirkel, 1972).[8] For example, Zirkel reported that Mahakian and Mitchell found scores on the Otis Group Intelligence Scale to be significantly higher among Spanish-speaking children in the primary grades when instructions were given in Spanish as compared to when instructions were given in English. However, Anastasi and Cordova, using the Cattel Culture Free Test, did not find language of instruction to be a significant factor with Spanish-speaking children. A more positive note is offered by Moreno (1970), who did a literature review of studies specifically investigating the effects of bilingualism on the measurement of intelligence of elementary school children. He concluded that "in general, the findings of the studies tend to support the conclusion that monolingual Spanish speakers and bilingual children suffer from a language handicap when intelligence is measured on verbal testing."

Sánchez said that tests were tools that could be used to find educational needs but questioned the value of IQ tests as yardsticks of intelligence for bilingual children; for example, Binet tests contain many words not in the recommended word lists for bilingual children, in addition to other qualitative variables (e.g. experiences, background, rapport, etc.) presupposed by these tests. Supplying word knowledge, he felt, would not necessarily remove the language handicap.[9]

García (1972) questioned many of the intrinsic assumptions underlying the basic structure of the Stanford-Binet IQ test and concluded these assumptions are so restrictive that to use these scores to compare groups is tantamount to a social conspiracy to label these groups inferior and propagate the status quo. Binet built the test on the assumption of general intelligence which, at the start, affected the choice of items; secondly, only items having to do with reading, writing, and arithmetic were included. The standardization sample included only children with Anglo, English-speaking parents. If one were to write items that favored Chicanos, we would have equal IQs between Anglos and Chicanos, as male and female IQs are now equal as a result of designing it into the test.

Professor Sánchez stated that the fundamental questions in the use of mental tests among bilingual children were those of validity: 1. "Do the tests measure *in that particular child* what they purport to measure? The tests may be valid for the 'average' child and still lack validity for an individual or for a particular group. Questions of culture, schooling, socioeconomic status, etc., loom big in this phase of the problem;" 2. "Are the assumptions on which the test was based for the original 'norm' children applicable with equal justice to the particular case? If the use of a radio were assumed to sample intelligence, would a Navajo Indian living in a hogan be equally subject to such an assumption as average children, or would the tallying of sheep be a more desirable measure." Sánchez's emphasis on validity directed attention to the misinterpretation of test results among minorities.

On one occasion he discussed a study where about 1,000 Spanish-speaking children from communities in Texas, Colorado, and New Mexico were tested and obtained a median IQ of 78, slightly above the "moron" level of 70. Uncritical evaluation of test results could lead to the conclusion that the Spanish-speaking children represented by this large sample were capable of operating only at a level slightly above that of the "moron"; such a conclusion would be indefensible but such were the results of test application. A consideration of validity would show that the interpretation of the obtained median IQ of 78 (slightly above the moron level) depended on the extent to which the past histories of the Spanish-speaking children had been assayed by the test in equal manner, with equal justice, and in equal terms as the past histories of those children in the standardization sample.

George Sánchez stated that the school had the responsibility to supply those experiences to the child which would make those experiences sampled by standard measures as common to him as they were to those on whom the norms of the measures were based. When the school had met the language, cultural, disciplinary, and informational lacks of the child and the child had reached the saturation point of his capacity in the assimilation of fundamental experiences and activities—then failure on his part to respond to tests of such experiences and activities could be considered his failure. As long as the tests did not sample in equal degree a state of saturation that was equal for the 'norm' children and the particular bilingual child, it could not be assumed that the test was a valid one for that child. The Office for Civil Rights in the Department of Health, Education, and Welfare used this idea in drafting a recent policy statement.

On May 25, 1970, the Office for Civil Rights, HEW, issued a memorandum focusing on the identification of discrimination and denial of services on the basis of national origin. This memorandum was mailed to school districts with more than 5 percent national origin-minority group children and listed the following areas of concern relating to compliance with Title VI of the Civil Rights Act of 1964:

1. Where inability to speak and understand the English language excludes national origin-minority group children from effective participation in the educational program offered by a school district, the district must take affirmative steps to rectify the language deficiency in order to open its instructional program to these students.
2. School districts must not assign national origin-minority group students to classes for the mentally retarded on the basis of criteria which essentially measure or evaluate English language skills; nor may school districts deny national origin-minority group children access to college preparatory courses on a basis directly related to the failure of the school system to inculcate English language skills.
3. Any ability grouping or tracking system employed by the school system to deal with the special language skill needs of national origin-minority group children must be designed to meet such language skill needs as soon as possible and must not operate as an educational dead-end or permanent track.
4. School districts have the responsibility to adequately notify national origin-minority group parents of school activities which are called to the attention of other parents. Such notice in order to be adequate may have to be provided in a language other than English.

Gerry (1972), Office for Civil Rights official, stated the following regarding this memorandum:

The drafting of the policy statement (Memorandum to School Districts) reflected the operational philosophy that school districts should create a culturally relevant educational approach to assure equal access of all children to its full benefits. The burden, according to this philosophy, should be on the school to adapt its education approach so that the culture, language and learning style of all children in the school (not just those of Anglo, middle class background) are accepted and valued. Children should not be penalized for cultural and linguistic differences nor should they bear a burden to conform to a school sanctioned culture by abandoning their own.

He also stated that:

In the twenty-two months since the issuance of the May 25 Memorandum, the Department of Health, Education, and Welfare has developed a comprehensive program for implementation in the field. Techniques for proving noncompliance with the various sections of the Memorandum have been developed and field tested and have passed legal muster. New issues are being investigated as training programs make operational these investigative and analytical techniques.

This work of the Office for Civil Rights is one of the very few Federal civil rights efforts given a positive evaluation by the U.S. Commission on Civil Rights. Generally, the Federal effort was found to be "highly inadequate" (U.S. Commission on Civil Rights, 1973).

López (1973) reviewed and synthesized six letters of noncompliance sent by OCR to school districts found to be in noncompliance with one or more of the various sections of the memorandum.[10] Although the letters were small in number, they did provide the following information: a. a wide geographic overview, i.e., Massachusetts, Wisconsin, Arizona, Texas, and Indiana; b. a look at rural versus urban (Karnes City, Texas/East Chicago, Indiana) school districts; and c. a look at discriminatory treatment of a number of racial-ethnic groups, including the Spanish-speaking, American Indian, and blacks.

The following is a summary of the civil rights violations listed in the six civil rights noncompliance letters: 1. less adequate and effective educational services to minority students; 2. discriminatory assignment to and segregation of minority students in classes for the educable mentally retarded; 3. discrimination in class assignments (e.g. tracking) of minority students; 4. creation and operation of racially identifiable school or school sub-systems; 5. discrimination in the hiring of minority professional staff; 6. provision of less effective guidance and counseling services for minority students; 7. failure to notify parents in their primary language of school related matters; 8. discriminatory assignment of penalties for school violations among minority students. Table 1 shows civil rights violations by school district.

López also found review findings to mirror national statistics in several areas including deficiencies in English language skills at the first grade level among minority students, a progressive decline in educational performance among minorities, and over-representation of minorities in low-ability tracks and classes for the mentally retarded.

TABLE 1. Civil rights violations by school districts

| Violations | \multicolumn{6}{c}{Districts} |
| --- | --- | --- | --- | --- | --- | --- |
|  | 1 | 2 | 3 | 4 | 5 | 6 |
| 1. Less adequate and effective educational services to minority students | X | X | X | X | X | X |
| 2. Discriminatory assignment to and segregation of minority students in EMR classes | X | X |  | X | X |  |
| 3. Discrimination in class assignments (e.g. tracking) | X | X |  |  | X | X |
| 4. Creation and operation of racially identifiable schools or school sub-systems |  |  | X | X | X |  |
| 5. Discrimination in the hiring of minority professional staff |  | X |  |  | X | X |
| 6. Provision of less effective guidance and counseling services for minority students |  | X |  |  |  | X |
| 7. Failure to notify parents in their primary language of school-related matters | X |  |  |  |  |  |
| 8. Discriminatory assignment of penalties among minorities students for school violations |  | X |  |  |  |  |

Civil rights violations are rank-ordered according to frequency of occurrence starting at the top with the most frequent. Key to school district above:
1. East Chicago Public Schools
2. Shawano, Wisconsin Joint District #8
3. Boston Public School System
4. Winslow Public Schools
5. Uvalde Independent School District
6. Karnes City Independent School District

## Discussion

If schools use mental tests to determine the capability of students, and if these tests do not, in fact, measure these capabilities and yet are used uncritically as yardsticks of intelligence, obviously, students who do not measure up to the "norms" are placed at a disadvantage and, therefore, will receive less than an equal opportunity in their educational endeavor.

Dr. George Sánchez spent a great deal of his professional career, beginning in the 1930s, investigating the issues surrounding mental testing of minorities, and in particular, the Spanish-speaking. He sought to insure equal educational opportunities for all children. He was among the first spokesmen for bilingual and bi-cultural education. His voice was loudly heard in academic circles. He influenced, eventually, public policy in and out of the government and throughout the public school system.

His objectivity in the heredity-versus-environment issue, his emphasis on the validation of tests, and his insistence that school districts in the United States take the responsibility of educating minority children before making judgments of mental inferiority, provided an important base for those who have followed him in the quest for equal educational opportunities for all children.

## NOTES

1. The important question here is whether or not subordinate groups are genetically inferior to Anglos in intelligence because they as a group score lower than Anglos on mental tests.
2. Sánchez was one of the first to warn that English-language IQ tests were questionable.
3. Language differences may play a role in the adjustment of Chicano children to school (Sattler, 1970).
4. The Office for Civil Rights, Department of Health, Education, and Welfare has documented cases where school districts have failed to inculcate English-language skills (López, 1973).
5. Jensen states that 80 percent of the variance on IQ among Anglos is genetic variance (1970).
6. (1) Since genetic influences probably have an effect on mental functioning, differences in IQ are primarily determined by heredity; (2) the closer the genetic relationship between two people, the more similar their IQ; (3) social class is correlated with IQ because biologically more intelligent people rise in social class.
7. (1) Less than 1.4 per room; (2) mother expects the child to get some college; (3) the head of the household has nine plus years of education; (4) the family speaks English all or most of the time; (5) the family owns their own home.
8. These reviews include studies using translated tests (i.e., Spanish and English versions), where test instructions are either in Spanish or English, and where verbal and "nonverbal" mental measurements are compared.
9. Consider the added difficulty of homonyms, word usage, and equivalency of concepts and organized ideas.
10. According to one OCR official, these six letters were part of twenty-one letters of noncompliance that had been mailed as of Fall 1972. By this time there were also approximately thirty-six additional districts under review. The six letters were all that were available from OCR.

## BIBLIOGRAPHY

García, J., "IQ: The Conspiracy," *Psychology Today*, (September, 1972), pp. 40–43.

GERRY, M. H., "Cultural Freedom and the Rights of La Raza," (unpublished, 1972).
JENSEN, A. R., "Can We and Should We Study Race Differences?" in J. Hellmuth ed., *Disadvantaged Child*, Vol. 3: "Compensatory Education: A National Debate," (New York: Brunner/Mazel, 1970), pp. 124–157.
KAGAN, J. "The IQ Puzzle: What Are We Measuring," *Inequality in Education*, (1973), pp. 5–13.
LÓPEZ, R. E., "A Review and Synthesis of Six Civil Rights Noncompliance Letters Sent to Elementary and Secondary School Districts by the Health, Education, and Welfare Office for Civil Rights," (unpublished, 1973).
MERCER, J. R., "Sociocultural Factors in the Educational Evaluation of Black and Chicano Children." Presented at the 10th Annual Conference on Civil and Human Rights of Educators and Students, (Washington, D.C.: February 18–20, 1972).
MORENO, S., "Problems Related to Present Testing Instruments," *El Grito*, (1970), pp. 135–139.
SATTLER, J., "Chapter 20: Testing Minority Group Children," prepublication copy, 1972, (3)1–(3)57.
U.S. COMMISSION ON CIVIL RIGHTS, *The Federal Civil Rights Enforcement Effort—a Reassessment*, (Washington, D.C.: U.S. Commission on Civil Rights, January, 1973).
ZIRKEL, P.A., "Spanish-speaking Students and Standardized Tests," *Urban Review*, (Spring, 1972).

# George Sánchez:
# Teacher, Scholar, Activist

**CAREY McWILLIAMS**

It was not my good fortune to know George Sánchez well personally; our meetings were infrequent, separated by long intervals, and our correspondence was limited. Nevertheless I thought of him—and still think of him—as a close personal friend, a tribute no doubt to his generosity, kindness, and responsiveness. His death saddened me to a degree which made me realize how much I liked and admired him and how much his friendship had meant to me.

    In the spring of 1942—April 27-30, I attended a conference held at the University of New Mexico in Albuquerque which Dr. Joaquín Ortega had organized with, as I recall, the cooperation and assistance of certain government agencies including the Bureau of Indian Affairs and the Soil Conservation Service. The conference had to do with the Spanish-speaking of the Southwest, their problems and prospects and government policies related to their needs. I presented a paper and took part in the discussions. It was at this conference that I first met Dr. George I. Sánchez and came to know something about his background and career. I am not sure just when I first read *Forgotten People*, which was published in 1940, but whenever it was, the book made a deep and lasting impression on me. At this same conference, I also met for the first time Hugh Calkins of the Soil Conservation Service and Allen Harper of the Bureau of Indian Affairs, both of whom I came to hold in high esteem. Along with Dr. Eshref Shevky, they were responsible for the important Tewa Basin studies. Allen Harper and I became and remained close friends until his untimely death. Calkins I do not remember meeting again, but I had occasion to admire his astute direction of the Soil Conservation Service in New Mexico and his remarkable insights into the problems of the region. At the close of the conference, my wife and I were taken on a tour of some of the Spanish-speaking villages between Santa Fe and Taos, including Truchas and Cordova, an extraordinary experience for us and one of which I still retain vivid memories.

The Albuquerque conference and attendant experiences, including long talks with the participants, was, in a sense, my first direct exposure to the Spanish-speaking villages of New Mexico and their inhabitants. Of course I wanted to know more about the people, the setting, and the region, including its history and present-day socioeconomic-political realities. The individuals I met at the conference, and Dr. Sánchez in particular, proved to be excellent guides and advisers, patient, knowledgeable, and rich in insights. Prior to this visit, I had for a long time been interested in Chicanos in California, their history, work experience, problems, and relationships; but I had not fully sensed the way in which the New Mexico "chapter" fitted into the larger experience of the Spanish-speaking until this visit. But I lost little time in attempting to learn more about the "forgotten people" of New Mexico, Colorado, and Texas. And when my friend, Louis Adamic, asked me to contribute a volume on the Spanish-speaking to the "Peoples of America" series he was editing for Lippincott, I made good use of the knowledge and insights of those who had participated in the Albuquerque conference. Of these sources I was more indebted to George Sánchez and Allen Harper (on the Indian connection) than to any of the other participants.

In the spring of 1951, not long after my book *North From Mexico: The Spanish-Speaking People of the United States* was first published, I left Southern California to join the staff of *The Nation*—succeeding to the editorship in 1955—and have since lived in New York. Among other unpleasant consequences, this shift in residence made it difficult for me to maintain ties with friends and associates in the Southwest. In the process of transition, also, I made a gift of my library and certain papers and documents to the University of California at Los Angeles and—in the general confusion of moving—quite a lot of my correspondence was lost or misplaced, so that I cannot refer to my continuing correspondence with Sánchez. As a result of my tight working schedule, editing a weekly journal is a compulsive, time-consuming, never-ending task, and the location of *The Nation*, 20 Vesey Street, was quite a distance from the barrios of East Los Angeles and the mountain villages of New Mexico—so of necessity my involvement—but not my interest—in the affairs of the Spanish-speaking as well as direct contact with the friends I had met in the course of my writings on the subject, rapidly abated.

But from time to time I exchanged letters with George Sánchez and had occasion, more than once, to seek his advice about articles, book reviews, and editorials relating to the Spanish-speaking. His responses were invariably prompt, helpful, and to the point. On January 20-22, 1959, the National Council of the Protestant Episcopal Church held a conference in Austin on "Latin-American Relations in the Southwestern United States." Along with my friend Maury Maverick, Jr., and Sánchez, I participated in this conference and read a paper on "Good Neighbors, Good Friends," which appears in the summary of the conference and printed in pamphlet form. I am sure that George Sánchez was the moving force behind this conference and that he was, of course, responsible for my presence there. The conference gave us a chance to renew our friendship, and we made the most of the opportunity, limited as it was in point of time. Later we continued to correspond, but I do not remember seeing him again.

George Sánchez was more than a remarkable scholar and distinguished educator. He was a forceful and courageous leader, a brilliant spokesman for the Spanish-speaking, and the constant foe of cant and hypocrisy. Only educators can properly appraise his pioneer work in attempting to educate "Anglo" educators about the educational problems of children from Spanish-speaking homes and communities. His efforts in this field alone were heroic and his achievements will stand as a lasting monument to his name and reputation. I knew him as a friend, and a good friend he proved to be. He was a prime source of whatever insight I managed to acquire as a non-Spanish-speaking "Anglo"—albeit one of very mixed ancestry—into the fascinating experience of the Spanish-speaking of the Southwest, an experience that is now taking on new dimensions of interest and importance for the culture of the region. An editorial which I wrote for *The Nation* (June 5, 1972) after his death summarizes some of the reasons why I cherish my friendship with George Sánchez:

> Washington has its full share of memorials for national heroes—explorers, generals, admirals, presidents, statesmen—whose reputations have been certified, sanctified, and recorded in song and

story and first-grade readers. But what Washington does not have, and needs, is a People's Pantheon, a memorial to those men and women who never attained widespread national fame but who served the true interests of the people better, in many cases, than the "official" heroes.

Consider, for example, Dr. George Sánchez, of the University of Texas, who died recently. Born in Albuquerque, Dr. Sánchez was educated in the elementary and secondary schools of New Mexico and Arizona and received degrees from the University of Texas and the University of California after graduating from the University of New Mexico. No one knew more about what was wrong with the education of Spanish-speaking children in the public schools of the Southwest, or did more to correct the stupid and inept teaching practices which mangled the education of so many of these youngsters for so many years. His performance in this one area was heroic and memorable.

All those who have written about the Spanish-speaking are indebted to Dr. Sánchez for his little book *Forgotten People* (1940), about the Spanish-speaking in New Mexico, a classic in the field. He also published important studies of the educational systems of Mexico and Venezuela, as well as a fine book, *The People: A Study of the Navajos* (1948). He served as educational specialist on the staff of the Coordinator for Inter-American Affairs and on the board of the Peace Corps when it was first established. But it was as professor of Latin American education from 1940 until his death that he gained national recognition as a teacher and scholar. Upon learning of his death, one of his many doctoral students commented, "I'm sorry for all the students who will never know him." His record at the University of Texas indicates that he supervised more than sixty-five masters' theses and some twenty-eight doctoral dissertations.

But he was a great deal more than a scholar. In the finest sense of the term, he was an activist. He made it possible for others to make the best use of his scholarly research, his remarkable experience and his shrewd insights. A generation of young Mexican-Americans who are now transforming the status of the Spanish-speaking have been, in a sense, taught by him even if they never studied with him. He was a man of rare courage and infectious high spirits who never hesitated to say what he thought about bigotry and prejudice and institutional stupidities; he was never in awe of the high and mighty. Rep. J. J. Pickle, speaking in the House on May 2, said of him: "He has served well the cause of Spanish-speaking peoples in this country and abroad. And in so doing he has served well his country and his fellow man everywhere." The Washington Establishment will erect no memorial to him but he deserves a place of honor in the People's Pantheon of the future.

# Jorge Isidoro Sánchez y Sánchez (1906-1972)

## AMÉRICO PAREDES

There is a publication called *Leaders in Education*, a hefty volume that contains the biographies of the leading men and women of the United States who have made their mark in the field of Education. If you should care to look under the letter "S" in the fourth and latest edition of *Leaders in Education* (New York, 1971), you might be surprised to find that the name of George I. Sánchez is not there. Suppose you go, then, to a similar publication, also functioning as a kind of honor roll for people in Education—*Who's Who in American Education* (Nashville, Tenn., 1968). Again you will find George Sánchez among the missing. On the other hand, Dr. Sánchez *is* included in *Who's Who in America* for 1972-73.

There are many explanations we might come up with, as to why George Sánchez has been considered distinguished enough to appear in a *Who's Who* devoted to Americans of all walks of life, while—apparently—he does not rate mention in similar rosters devoted exclusively to scholars in his own field. I shall not attempt to go into such pormenores, at least not now—except to note how typical this was of the man and of his life. He was always a maverick, a noncomformist. And he often made his academic colleagues extremely uncomfortable by saying exactly what he thought. Furthermore, he believed in putting his convictions into action. Such behavior did not make for him a bed of roses during his tenure at the University of Texas.

Chicanos everywhere have come to know about George Sánchez and some of the things he stood for, but I doubt that the

---

These remarks were read at a dinner honoring George Sánchez, at the California State University in Sacramento, December 8, 1972.

fullness of his contribution has been truly appreciated. The basic facts about his career are well known:

Jorge Isidoro Sánchez y Sánchez was born in Albuquerque, New Mexico, on October 4, 1906. His parents were Telésforo and Juliana Sánchez, and he came from the stock of the early colonizers of the area. He received his elementary and secondary education in the public schools of Arizona and New Mexico. In 1923, at the advanced age of seventeen, he became a rural school teacher and principal in Bernalillo County, New Mexico, working during the summers toward his B.A. degree at the University of New Mexico. In 1930, he received his bachelor's degree, and by that time he had advanced from principal to superintendent of his school district. After that, his other degrees came in quick succession.

Immediately after receiving his bachelor's he had his first sojourn in Texas, attending the University of Texas on a fellowship from the General Education Board. One year later, in 1931, he had completed his Master of Science degree in Educational Psychology and Spanish. From Texas he went to the University of California, Berkeley, where in 1934 he received his Doctor of Education degree in Educational Administration. During these same years, by the way—from 1930 to 1935— he also served as Director of the Division of Information and Statistics in the New Mexico State Department of Education. An underachiever he was not.

During the period from 1935 to 1940 George Sánchez was, among other things, an Associate Professor of Education at the University of New Mexico, a Julius Rosenwald Research Associate, and Asesor Técnico General for the Ministerio de Educación Nacional of the Republic of Venezuela. Then, in 1940, he went to Texas to stay. From 1940 until his death on April 5, 1972, he was a Professor in the Department of History and Philosophy of Education (now Department of Cultural Foundations of Education), and Consultant in Latin American Education at the University of Texas. From 1951 to 1959, he was chairman of his department. As a teacher he gave of himself unstintingly to his students. He was still teaching during the spring semester of 1972, a few weeks before his death. During his tenure at the University of Texas, students of all interests and disciplines were drawn to his classes. As for his work as a graduate professor, it is officially reported that as a member of the UT Graduate Faculty he supervised more than 65 master's theses and 28 doctoral dissertations. He was a Visiting Professor at a number of universities in this country and abroad, and in 1967 he was awarded the honorary degree, Doctor of Laws, by the University of New Mexico, his alma mater.*

George Sánchez's bibliography is voluminous. The books, monographs, and special reports that he authored or edited during his lifetime run to something like fifty items, to which must be added some eighty articles that also came from his pen. The subjects that engaged his attention as author and editor range from the arithmetic of the ancient Mayas, through the culture of the Navajos, to education in southern Peru. But his overriding preoccupation was the quality of education given to children of Mexican descent in the United States. His many writings on the subject have made his name familiar to today's Chicanos, who see in him something of a precursor—one of the few glimmers of light in the dark days before the movimiento. Perhaps his best known work, certainly the one most frequently found in Mexican American bibliographies, is *Forgotten People*, a study that appeared in 1940 calling attention to the plight of Chicanos in New Mexico. But somewhat earlier, Sánchez was already attacking the validity of intelligence tests as applied to Chicano children. His best known articles on the subject are "Group Differences and Spanish-speaking Children: A Critical Review," which appeared in the *Journal of Applied Psychology* in 1932; and "Bilingualism and Mental Measures: A Word of Caution," published in the same journal in 1934.

Sánchez's writings are enough to earn him a favored place among the prominent figures our people have produced. However, to know only George Sánchez's published works is to know but part of the man. What is missing from such a picture is by far the most dynamic aspect of the man he was, and the most important one as far as his legacy to Mexican Americans of today and of the future. This aspect of Sánchez's work still awaits some thorough and basic research on the part of Chicano scholars of the present generation. We can, however, outline the major area of his activities, as they were readily apparent to those who knew the man for any length of time. Vital in our appreciation of George Sánchez is the recognition of his pioneer work in what we now call Mexican American Studies or Chicano Studies. We have said it is officially reported that Sánchez supervised some

---

*"Documents and Minutes of the General Faculty, University of Texas," September 27, 1972.

90 theses and dissertations during his tenure at Texas. Someone should make a survey of these theses and dissertations, noting how many of them deal not only with the Chicano's education but with his history and his culture. It is a safe bet that the proportion falling into this category will be high, because Sánchez understood education as extending into all of a people's activities. His tendency to range far and wide in interdisciplinary fields was one of the reasons why he was something of a thorn in the side of those who favored the academic status quo.

The courses Sánchez taught were influenced by this same point of view regarding the unity of education and culture. For many years at the University of Texas, he offered courses such as "The Social Context of Education," a fourth-year level course, and "Spanish-Speaking People and Their Acculturation in the United States," on the graduate level. So George Sánchez was teaching Mexican American Studies courses at Texas long before the idea of a Mexican American Studies program had come to anyone's attention. It was only natural, when Mexican American Studies were formally initiated at the University of Texas in 1970, that the courses taught by George Sánchez should become an important part of our program—a program they had preceded by many years.

The program at Texas drew strength not only from the courses but from the man. Sánchez was by then in extremely poor health, but he consented to serve on the faculty-student committee for Mexican American Studies. In January 1972, less than three months before George Sánchez's death, the program became involved in difficulties with the University of Texas administration. One of the first to jump into the breach was Sánchez, with eloquent and abrasive letters to the administration and to the press. I visited him at his home a few days before he was hospitalized for the last time. His final advice to me was, "Give them hell."

This, by the way, reveals still another aspect of George Sánchez's career and personality: his passionate commitment to the things he believed in. He was both a scholar and a man of action. A full list of his consultantships, directorships, committee chairmanships, and membership on boards and commissions would cover many pages. A few examples should give us an idea of the range of his activities in the areas that interest us most.

In 1935 and 1936 he was surveying rural education in México, where bilingualism and biculturalism are expressed in terms of Spanish and an Indian language, rather than in terms of

Spanish and English; but with the same problems and the same potential. Back in this country, from 1941 to 1947 he was a member of the Committee on Teaching English as a Second Language; and in 1945 he became president of the Council on Education of Spanish-speaking People in the Southwest, a post he held until 1950. He was director of a Bilingual Migrant Workshop for the Colorado State Department of Education in 1957 and was consultant for the U.S. Office of Education Project on Bilingualism from 1957 to 1959. In 1952 he was a consultant on the Education of Migrants; and from 1957 until his death he was active in the Migrant Children's Fund—as a member of the board of directors from 1957 to 1959, and as vice president since 1960. From 1951 to 1959, he was director of the American Council of Spanish-speaking People. He also found time to be vice chairman of the Texas Council on Human Relations, a member of the board of directors of the Central Texas Affiliate of the American Civil Liberties Union, and president general of LULAC from 1941 to 1942.

These examples, lengthy though they may seem, are but a small part of the activities expressing his concern—decades before the Chicano movement—for human rights in general and for the rights of his people in particular. And let us make it clear that this list was not an exercise in vitaemanship. His activities in these organizations went beyond mere membership, or even polite participation. Sánchez could be blunt or caustic, and he very often was, in attempting to gain a hearing for significant action in education and civil rights. He was never one to condone window dressing. Another area of research that awaits some young Chicano scholar is in Sánchez's correspondence to people in high places both in the government and in academia. He did not believe in mincing words when he felt it necessary to speak out on issues. Still another area that he was active in was the legal battles for school desegregation in Texas. He often appeared as an expert witness in virtue of his standing as an educator. He was in the midst of this fight in 1948, during the historic case, Delgado vs. Bastrop Independent School District; and in 1971, just a few months before his death, he appeared as a witness in a case of *de facto* segregation of Chicano schoolchildren in Austin.

There were so many facets to the life and personality of George Sánchez that it is not easy to characterize him in a phrase or two. But if I were to attempt it, I would say of him that he was above all a fighter, a man of courage. Let me say that his was not the courage of the type that is called machismo, that supposedly

Mexican complex that social scientists love to study. Machismo is supposed to be something especially ours; after all, we are told, we do have a word for it. But we forget that the term machismo was coined fairly recently in our history, by social scientists. Mexican social scientists, it is true, but trained in North American methodologies. It is a strange commentary on the subtle ways of brainwashing that many of our young Chicano writers have accepted machismo as an ineluctable part of their ethnic make-up and, even more, have attempted to elevate the cult of the macho into a kind of Chicano mystique. The cult of the bully—the matón and the castigador de mujeres—does not deserve a place in our scale of values. On the other hand, the willingness to face death for a cause is not machismo. It is simply courage of a high order and has been admired by many peoples in many ages.

Curiously enough, there is another aspect of courage that people of Mexican culture have always admired—so much so that we *do* have a term for it. This kind of courage, which by the way has never interested people trying to psychoanalyze us en masse, is what we call *valor civil*. *Valor civil* is courage that requires no weapon but the will itself; it is the courage of the unarmed and peaceful citizen who will not flinch before threats of violence. *Valor civil* is the ability to stand steadfast for what you think is right, come what may. George Sánchez had *valor civil*. He was a fighter for the things he believed in—way back, many years ago, when very few fought alongside of him.

And he suffered for it. He faced threats of violence in his early days in New Mexico, and in later years pressures of various sorts were applied to him. For a long time—until the last few years of his life—he was one of the most poorly paid full professors at the University of Texas. In the same way, he fought against the physical ailments that afflicted him. A man with less courage would have retired from active life ten or twenty years before the end—if he had had to bear the burdens George Sánchez bore. But he was in the thick of things until the very last, giving of himself without stint—for which many thousands of us are grateful.

As you well know, one of the fictions we have had to contend with as Chicanos has been the legend of the sleeping giant who suddenly wakes up. As one of our recent advocates has put it, "That lazy bandido sleeping beneath the big sombrero in the shade of the adobe hut has suddenly awakened. . . ." Certainly the age of self-analysis and self-discovery has finally caught up with him.* With advocates like that, who needs detractors? The lives of men like George Sánchez are ample evidence that Chicanos were not asleep in the generations preceding this one. They have been awake to their problems for more than a century, and they have always been concerned with questions of self-analysis and identity.

Yet, those men—forerunners of the Chicano movement—were frustrated in their attempts to have sufficient impact on the majority society in order to bring about changes they desired as much as we desire them today. Some may argue that they did not create the necessary stir because they were a small minority of their own generation. But let us not forget how small a fraction of the Mexican-American population is formed by the Chicano activists of today.

If there is any group in the United States that "suddenly awakened into an age of self-analysis" during the 1960s, it is the WASP majority. And without taking credit away from our contemporary Chicano leaders, one may conjecture whether they would have been so successful in making themselves heard, had they not come along at the right time, when the American majority were willing to listen.

These remarks are intended, not as a captious observation on the recent past but as a hard look at the future. The sixties were indeed a time for soul searching among the majority in the United States. But the signs begin to point in other directions as we move deeper into the seventies. It begins to look more and more as though a reaction has set in, and—as regards minority rights and interests—no one really knows what the next few years may bring. After a period of relatively quick, though partial, successes in the sixties, we may be entering again into times when we will be able to inch forward toward our goals only at the cost of great effort and much frustration. In such times, we will need men patterned after Jorge Isidoro Sánchez y Sánchez.

---

*Edward Simmen, ed., *The Chicano: From Caricature to Self-Portrait* (New York, 1971), 15.

# Perspectives on the Chicano

**PAUL S. TAYLOR**

George I. Sánchez came from the oldest stream of European immigrants that settled in New Spain. In 1605 they arrived in what now we call the State of New Mexico. This was two years before the English settled in Virginia, and fifteen years before the Pilgrims landed at Plymouth Rock. More than two centuries passed until the progeny of these settlements met. Borne on the tides of history, it was the English language, culture, and economic and political power that swept westward from the Atlantic Coast to the Pacific, not the reverse. Yet these tides never obliterated Spanish language and culture in southwestern areas where they had taken root, nor in areas to which later they had spread.

The twentieth century brought renewed and heavy infusion of Spanish culture, language, and people into the Southwest. This fresh immigrant tide, coming from Mexico, not only expanded the numbers of persons with Spanish language and heritage but also diversified their racial and cultural strains. It spread widely into areas spotted over the United States, multiplying contacts with the dominant English-European elements of American society. Within the Spanish-Mexican societies a sense of community was to develop only slowly, awaiting the rise of an enlarged American-born generation.

George Sánchez was well aware of the distinctive characters of the two migration phases. Of the first—the impact of the westward sweep from the Atlantic—he wrote in 1967: "The Spanish American of New Mexico was left to the mercy of waves of exploiters: merchants, cattle barons, land grabbers, venal politicians—merciless all." Of the recent influx from México he wrote that "cheap labor displaces Americans of Spanish-Mexican descent all along the border, and even beyond." Searching for leadership among his own people, he presented a paper at the University of New Mexico entitled "The Default of Leadership." In it he observed that although some persons of his ancestry were beginning to receive the advantages of higher education, "These few were powerless to stem the overwhelming tide."[1]

In contrast to George Sánchez, who spoke from the insight of an insider, I can write only from the observations of an outsider. Born in the final decade of the nineteenth century of British and European ancestry, I had no contact with the Spanish-Mexican world until 1927. Then, as an observer, I was tossed for five years into the modern stream of immigration from México. This I followed in person from its sources in México to its agricultural and industrial destinations in California, Colorado, Illinois, Indiana, and Pennsylvania. Now, in this personal perspective of forty years, I meet a rising young generation of insiders of which Sánchez was a forerunner, a generation seeking to understand and evaluate the position of Chicanos in contemporary American society. I observe them endeavoring to find common bonds that can unite the diverse elements among them, the common values that can provide and clarify their goals. This can be the task only of insiders. But if insiders can give the answers, perhaps an outsider can assist by offering his observations and asking some of the questions.

Chicanos, like Europeans and unlike Africans, came to the United States by their own or their forebears' decisions. They have homogenized into this society more slowly than most Europeans, and much faster than Africans. For one thing, their own cultural and racial heritage is in large measure European. Then why have they shared the "melting pot" processes more slowly than most Europeans? Some answers can be suggested, relevant especially to the large numbers who entered the United States in the twentieth century from México.

The outbreak of World War I in 1914 cut off immigration from Europe. In the decade that followed, Congress sharply reduced permissible entries from Europe and excluded immigrants from large zones in Asia. U.S. entry into the war in 1917 stimulated the labor demands of the economy and reduced the supply of domestic labor by drawing many into the armed forces. This created a "forced draft" siphoning laborers in from México. These served mainly in western agriculture, on western railways, and to a lesser extent in northern industry.

Although immigrants from México came by their own decision, they did not make the decisions determining their social and economic role upon arrival in the United States. Rather, they responded to the decisions of others who sought their labor services. This points to a first question: When, in the stream of time, did these later Mexicans arrive, and what, consequently, were the roles into which they were fitted? Time, place, and occupation are elements crucial to understanding.

The place assigned them in the sugar beet industry at the time of their arrival offers one concrete illustrative answer. This agricultural industry sprang into existence at the beginning of the twentieth century and expanded rapidly on western irrigated lands and at points in the Middle West as far eastward as Michigan and Ohio. Already the era of free land had passed; a decade earlier this frontier had closed down. Opportunity for Mexicans to acquire farms of their own on which to grow sugar beets did not exist. The demand for their services was as laborers on the farms of others—north Europeans who had preceded them. It was limited to seasons of need for labor in the beet fields beyond the capacity of the farmer's family and his hired man to provide. For most Chicanos this meant northward migration to the beet fields in the spring, and southward migration to winter quarters—even return to México—in the fall.

This reception by the sugar beet industry—and it was similar in cotton as that crop expanded into Arizona and California under irrigation—was in sharp contrast to the spirit abroad in México at the time. Although they left México in an era when "tierra y libertad" expressed popular aspirations, their personal heritage generally was not that of peasants experienced in carrying the responsibilities of farm management. As field laborers at home they fitted readily into the role of migrant seasonal workers in the United States.

In other eras it would have been otherwise. Earlier immigrants entering by the Atlantic seaboard from the seventeenth through the nineteenth centuries had found "free land" awaiting them. These were largely English, Scotch, German, Irish, and Scandinavian in origin, and largely of peasant stock. With opportunity on the land open before them, they rose in large numbers by the "agricultural ladder" of the times, either directly to landownership, or step by step from hired man to tenant, to farmer laboring on his own land. Even Asian immigrants, especially those with peasant experience such as Japanese and Hindustanis arriving prior to World War I, were able to rise to tenancy and landownership in California and the West. The South was an exception, and a region generally avoided by free immigrants. There the large plantation system prevailed, resting on originally unfree African laborers denied access to land of their own.

Except in the Old South, times had changed greatly when the twentieth century Mexicans arrived. Not only was there no agricultural ladder for them to ascend; the effect of their ready availability to landowners was to check further widespread distribution of landownership, and so to contribute to the decline of the "family farm."[2]

Participation of Mexicans in the historic melting pot process by which immigrants were amalgamated into the receiving society was further slowed by the very proximity of México, their country of origin. Since it was immediately adjacent geographically, it was also close psychologically in the minds of Mexican immigrants in the United States. Return to the mother country was natural and easy, or seemed so whether actually undertaken or merely contemplated. Either way, the result was reflected in slowness to seek U.S. citizenship and to engage in active participation in the civic life of the United States. These actions were retarded for a full generation and more. As with the Japanese-Americans, World War II, with its draft calls for military service, confronted the new U.S.-born generation with tangible questions: Was their future to be U.S. citizens? Was Mexican heritage to override full allegiance to the country of their birth and residence? Or might there be some balance between these alternatives?

Earlier European immigrants to the United States seldom faced such questions. Over the centuries, especially as long as travel was by sailing vessel, decision to emigrate to America was accepted as final, with no anticipation of return to the homeland, not even for a visit. Only later, in the days of large and fast passenger steamships did frequently homing "birds of passage" appear. This change was notable among Italians in years immediately preceding World War I. Many of them came to the United States for industrial employment, returned to Italy when employment slackened, and came again to the United States when "good times" and jobs reappeared. Many Mexicans did likewise.

Among the results of delay by Mexicans in deciding to accept and affirm American citizenship has been prolonged civic inaction to protect their own self-interest. A dramatic example is the survival—under very dubious legality—of concentrated landownership in Imperial Valley, California. There the Bureau of Reclamation constructed the Boulder Canyon Project to serve irrigation needs of the valley. Reclamation law was declared to "govern the construction, operation, and management" of the works "except as otherwise . . . provided."[3] In order to distribute water and land "in accordance with the greatest good to the greatest number of individuals," as described by the U.S. Supreme Court, reclamation law allows no water deliveries in excess of 160 acres per individual landowner. The project was authorized in 1928, yet in 1965 some 800 persons owned and were receiving water on 233,000 acres, an average of 290 acres apiece.

One-third of the valley's population is of Mexican ancestry, consisting almost entirely of landless field laborers. Hardly any are independent farmers. Reflecting these facts, the overwhelming majority of "farm personnel" in Imperial Valley—87.3 percent—belongs to the "lower class," as compared with only 13.6 percent in Iowa where, historically, landownership has been widely distributed.[4] The purpose of acreage limitation on water deliveries and a companion requirement of residence on the part of the water receiver, is to prevent the very stratification that has developed in Imperial Valley under nonenforcement of the law, with Mexicans at the bottom.

In 1933 a Secretary of the Interior said that acreage limitation law does not apply to Imperial Valley. In 1945 a Solicitor of Interior said that it does, and in 1957 a Solicitor General of the United States said the same. Still, there was no enforcement. In 1964, thirty-one years after the first Secretary said acreage limitation law does not apply, a second Secretary said that it does. When finally the case reached district court in 1971, a first judge agreed with the 1933 Secretary that the law does not apply. Thereupon the Justice Department dropped its own case without appeal, allowing the adverse decision to stand. This appeared to close the door of opportunity that a law designed to provide "land for the landless" sought to open, i.e., "tierra y libertad."

Over virtually all these years there is no evidence that Mexican-Americans were informed, consulted, or concerned over the outcome. Except for the arrival in the valley of a Brooklyn physician, this would have been the end of opportunity for the many on Imperial Valley land. This practitioner of medicine in time became curious about this situation, investigated its legal aspects, gathered about himself 123 Chicanos lacking farms, and brought suit to have the law enforced.

The initial response by the court was discouraging: the district judge who denied that the law applies to Imperial Valley, denied also the right of a physician and landless Chicanos to appeal his decision. In August, 1973, however, the Ninth Circuit Court of Appeals reversed this latter denial and agreed to hear the landless in their own behalf.[5]

The slowness of Mexicans over so many years to act in their own self-interest through the judiciary is paralleled by the more recent fact that so far, apparently, no organization of Chicanos has undertaken to publicly endorse the suit and the issue it stands for, or to raise funds for its prosecution through the courts. Explanation of the answer to the natural question, Why not? must be deepseated, rather than accidental.

To begin with, there is lack of a close sense of unity among Chicanos, a lack grounded on both historical and contemporary facts. In the late nineteen twenties when I was observing Mexican laborers in the field, I found no generally recognized word or phrase all-inclusive of the various groups of persons of Mexican ancestry in the Southwest. "Texas-Mexicans" (Tejanos) were distinguished from "Spanish Americans" of New Mexico and southern Colorado, and from the newly arrived "Mexicans." To the latter, the Spanish Americans were "little brothers" (hermanitos). This fractionized condition apparently has not wholly vanished despite current prevalence of the all-embracing terms "Chicanos" and "la raza."

At the end of the nineteen sixties, careful students of Mexicans cautiously reported progress in the direction of a developing sense of unity that I found so conspicuously absent in the nineteen twenties. They concluded:

> Mexican Americans began to discover *themselves* at about the same time that the nation noticed their existence. The changes they witnessed in the larger society solidified a growing conviction that their traditional approach of patiently waiting for recognition was unproductive. Mexican Americans formed politically oriented organizations *demanding* national attention. A new generation of leaders began to sense that the whole complex of national opinion, concern within the Federal government, and modern communications media could be used to voice and eventually redress their grievances. The concept of a "national minority" was slowly replacing the parochial orientation of earlier spokesmen who sought to solve individual problems in individual areas.[6]

Final answers to the questions that face Mexicans are unlikely at this time. Each future generation will face these and ask others, and will give answers revised in the light of its own time.

## NOTES

1. George I. Sánchez, *Forgotten People*, (1967).
2. P. S. Taylor, "Hand Laborers in the Sugar Beet Industry," *Agricultural History*, Vol. 41 (1967), p. 19.
3. 43 United States Code 617m. (1928).
4. T. Lynn, Smith, "A Study of Social Stratification in the Agricultural Sections of the United States . . . ," *Rural Sociology*, Vol. 34, 496 (1969), pp. 506-508. Yellen *vs.* Hickel, 352 F. Supp. 1300 (S. D. Calif. 1972).
5. Lyle W. Robinson, "Brave Ben Yellen," *Chicago Jewish Forum*, 27, 22 (1968); Michael Kinsley, "Ben Yellen's Fine Madness," *Washington Monthly*, 2, 11 (1971), p. 28; P. S. Taylor, "Water, Land, and Environment. Imperial Valley: Law Caught in the Winds of Politics," *Natural Resources Journal*, 13, 1 (1973). Eric Mankin, "The Man Who Stands up to Agribusiness," *Mother Jones*, Vol. 2, No. 2 (1977), pp. 30-35.
6. Leo Grebler, Joan W. Moore, and Ralph C. Guzman, *The Mexican-American People: The Nation's Second Largest Minority* (1970), p. 4.

# A Bibliography of George I. Sánchez

**JAMES N. MOWRY**

The bibliography that follows is ordered chronologically. This strategy was adopted so that readers could obtain a sketch of Dr. Sánchez's active life by observing the time sequenced topics of his written works. Reading these publications in chronological sequence is experiencing vicariously the drama of the life of a man dedicated to elevating the quality of human relationships. Dr. Sánchez was a striking example of a rare wholeness—scholarship and action directed toward the satisfaction of human need.

In his publications he sought to break through erroneous generalizations that inhibited social interaction and appreciation of cultural differences. He attempted to replace those generalizations with fuller understanding of historical and cultural factors that contribute to diversity. He tried to clarify the meaning of democratic social arrangements, particularly in education, and suggested means of bringing about needed reconstruction. He identified economic, social, political, health, and educational needs and goals of minority groups and documented the roadblocks that impeded progress toward fulfillment of those needs and goals. His attitude was positive in the suggestions he recommended for the removal of obstacles to improvement of social welfare.

At times his writings reflected the anger and indignation he must have felt when confronted by the reality of entrenched bigotry and cultural blindness of special interest groups in the dominant culture that manipulated our institutions to the disadvantage of American minority groups, particularly the Spanish-speaking people in the Southwest. But as the record will show, he never doubted the potential good of democratic ideals as guides for social interaction nor the intentions of the majority of Americans to bring these ideals closer to reality through social unity amid cultural diversity.

## BOOKS AND MONOGRAPHS

"A Study of the Scores of Spanish-Speaking Children on Repeated Tests," Masters Thesis, University of Texas, Austin, Texas, 1931.

"Age-Grade Status of the Rural Child in New Mexico," *Educational Research Bulletin 1*, 1 (Albuquerque: New Mexico Department of Education, November 1932).

"The Education of Bilinguals in a State School System," Doctoral Dissertation, University of California, Berkeley, April 1934.

*Mexico: A Revolution By Education*, (New York: The Viking Press, 1936).

"Equalization of Educational Opportunities," The University of New Mexico Bulletin 347. (Albuquerque: University of New Mexico Press, December 1939).

*Forgotton People*, (Albuquerque: University of New Mexico Press, 1940).

with F. R. Wickham and A. L. Campa, *Practical Handbook of Spanish Commercial Correspondence*. Inter-American Series, Occasional Papers. (New York: The Macmillan Company, 1943).

*The Development of Higher Education in Mexico*, (New York: Kings Crown Press, 1944).

with P. Cutright and W. W. Charter, *Latin America: Twenty Friendly Nations*. Inter-American Series, Occasional Papers. (New York: The Macmillan Company, 1944).

*First Regional Conference on the Education of Spanish-Speaking People in the Southwest*, Inter-American Series, Occasional Papers. (Austin: University of Texas Press, March 1946).

with H. J. Otto, et al. *A Guide for Teachers of Spanish-Speaking Children*, Bulletin 464, (Austin: Texas State Department of Education, 1946).

with Eleanor Delaney, *Spanish Gold*, Inter-American Series, Occasional Papers. (New York: The MacMillan Company, 1946).

with Clarice T. Wittenburg, *Materials Relating to the Education of Spanish-Speaking People*, Inter-American Series, Occasional Papers. (Austin: University of Texas Press, February 1948).

"The People": *A Study of the Navajos*, (Washington, D.C.: United States Indian Service, 1948).

with R. C. Reindorp and Bernice M. Boswell, *References for Teachers of English as a Foreign Language*, Inter-American Series, Occasional Papers, (Austin: University of Texas Press, September 1949).

*"Wetback": A Preliminary Report*, made to the Advisory Committee for the Study of Spanish-Speaking People, (Austin: University of Texas Press, June 1949).

*Age of Discovery: Spanish and Portuguese Exploration*, (Chicago: Coronet Instructional Films, 1950).

*Concerning Segregation of Spanish-Speaking Children in the Public Schools*, Inter-American Series, Occasional Papers, (Austin: University of Texas Press, December 1951).

with Marie Hughes, "Learning A New Language," *The 1957-58 General Service Bulletin* 101, (Washington, D.C.: Association for Childhood Education, 1958).

with Howard L. Putnam, *Materials Relating To The Education Of Spanish-Speaking People: An Annotated Bibliography*, (Austin: University of Texas Press, 1959).

with Charles L. Eastlack, *Say It The Spanish Way*, (Austin: Good Neighbor Commission of Texas, 1960).

*Arithmetic in Maya*, Published privately, (Austin, Texas, 1961).

with Luisa G. Sánchez, *Education in Southern Peru: A Report*, (Limited private edition for USAID, Austin, 1962).

The Development of Education in Venezuela, (Washington, D.C.: U. S. Department of Health, Education and Welfare, Office of Education, 1963).

*México*, (Boston: Ginn & Co., 1965).

## ARTICLES AND SECTIONS IN BOOKS

"Analysis of Teachers' Salaries in New Mexico," *New Mexico School Review*. (March 1932), pp. 18-25.

"Scores of Spanish-Speaking Children on Repeated Tests," *Pedagogical Seminary and Journal of Genetic Psychology*, (March 1932), pp. 223-231.

"Teachers' Salaries Cost Less Today Than They Did a Decade Ago," *New Mexico School Review*, (March 1932), pp. 30-31.

"Educational Research in New Mexico," *Journal of Educational Research*, (April-May 1932), pp. 331-332.

# A BIBLIOGRAPHY

"False Economy in School Budgets," *New Mexico Press*, (April 2, 1932).

"Cost Distribution for Education in New Mexico," *U. S. Daily*, (April 8, 1932).

"Blanket Cuts in School Budgets," *New Mexico School Review*, (May 1932), p. 6.

"Status of New Mexico in Educational Efficiency," *New Mexico State Tribune*, (May 19, 1932).

"Civic Insurance as Element of Education," *U. S. Daily*, (May 31, 1932).

"Responsibility for Curtailments," *New Mexico Press*, (June 29, 1932).

"Are Schoolmen 'Educational Politicos'?," *Albuquerque Tribune*, (October 14, 1932).

"Dr. Seyfried's Research into School Law and into School Finance," *New Mexico School Review*, (October 1932), pp. 23-24.

"Group Differences and Spanish-Speaking Children: A Critical Review," *Journal of Applied Psychology* 16, 5 (October 1932), pp. 549-558.

"New Mexico Studies," *Journal of Educational Research* 26, 6 (February 1933), pp. 477-478.

"Problemas de la educación de niños bilingues en los E. E. U. U.," *Sociedad Mexicana de Geografía y Estadística*, Centennial Publication. Mexico, (March 1933).

"A Compendium of the Educational Laws Enacted by the Eleventh Legislature," *New Mexico School Review*, (March 1933), pp. 20-23.

"The Referenda and School Finance," *New Mexico Press*, (May 17, 1933).

"Future Legislative Program for Financing Public Instruction in New Mexico," *University of New Mexico Bulletin*, (July 1934), pp. 96-105.

"Comment on J. R. McCollum's Paper," *University of New Mexico Bulletin*, (July 1934), pp. 117-120.

with Virgie Sánchez, "Education in Mexico in the Sixteenth Century," *The New Mexico Quarterly* 4, 3 (August 1934), pp. 184-192.

"Management and Mismanagement in a State Business: Education," *New Mexico Business Review*, (October 1934), pp. 132-137.

"Our Money's Worth," *The Taxpayer*, (November 17, 1934).

"Bilingualism and Mental Measures," *Journal of Applied Psychology* 8, 6 (December 1934), pp. 765–772.

"The Implications of a Basal Vocabulary to the Measurement of the Abilities of Bilingual Children," *Journal of Social Psychology* 5 (1934), pp. 395–402.

"Financing Public Education in New Mexico," *New Mexico School Review* 14, 5 (January 1934), pp. 4–7.

"Digest of Educational Laws Enacted by the Twelfth Legislature," *New Mexico School Review*, (March 1934), pp. 19–35.

"Child Development in the Rural Environment," in *Growth and Development: The Basis for Educational Programs*, (New York: Progressive Education Association, 1936), pp. 112–118.

"Theory and Practice in Rural Education," *Progressive Education* 13, 8 (1936), pp. 590–596.

"The Community School in the Rural Scene," Chapter 5 of *The Community School*, (Samuel Everett, Ed. New York: D. Appleton-Century Company, 1939), pp. 164–215.

"The State Public School Equalization Fund in Law and Practice," *New Mexico Business Review* 8 (January 1939), pp. 11–20.

"The Oil Industry and Education," in Papers presented at New Mexico Oil Conference, (Albuquerque: University of New Mexico Press, 1939), pp. 44–46.

"Education in Mexico," *The Annals of the American Academy of Political and Social Science* 208 (March 1940), pp. 144–152.

"Latin America and the Curriculum," *Curriculum Journal* 2, 7 (November 1940), pp. 303–306.

"Schools and Culture," *LULAC News*, (April 1940).

"Americanism," *LULAC News*, (October 1940).

"An Educational Philosophy to Meet the Needs of a Democracy in Crisis," *Proceedings of the Texas School Administration and Supervisors*, 8th Annual Mid-Winter Conference. (Austin, January 5, 1941), pp. 1–5.

"New Mexicans and Acculturation," *New Mexico Quarterly Review* 11, 1 (February 1941), pp. 61–68.

"Inter-American Education: Some Problems and an Opportunity," *Phi Delta Kappan* (November 1941), pp. 98–99.

"Educational Crisis in Mexico," *Butrava* 6, (February 1942), pp. 4–7.

"Cultural Relations within the Americas," *Childhood Education*, (April 1942), pp. 339–342.

# A BIBLIOGRAPHY

"Inter American Education: The New Frontier," in *Proceedings of the 46th National Congress of Parents and Teachers.* (San Antonio, 1942), pp. 33-40.

"North of the Border," in *Proceedings and Transactions of the Texas Academy of Science,* (Austin, 1942), pp. 77-85.

"Fundamental Problems in Education in Mexico," *The Educational Forum* 7, 4 (May 1943), pp. 321-327.

"Mexican Education as it Looks Today," *The Nation's Schools* 32, 3 (September 1943), p. 23.

"Pachucos in the Making," *Common Ground* 4, 1 (Autumn 1943), pp. 13-20.

with M. B. Lourenco Filho. "Education" in *Handbook of Latin American Studies: 1942, No. 8,* (Cambridge: Harvard University Press, 1943), pp. 161-167.

"Mexico in Transition," in *Proceedings of the Conference on Latin America in Social and Economic Transition,* (Albuquerque: University of New Mexico Press, 1943), pp. 95-97.

"Los problemas fundamentales de la Educación en México," *Educación Nacional.* (México, February 1944), pp. 56-60.

"Education of Minority and Special Groups in Rural Areas, *The White House Conference on Rural Education,* (October 1944), pp. 176-177.

"Education in Mexico," in *Encyclopedia of Modern Education,* (New York: American Association on Indian Affairs, Inc., 1944), pp. 15-25.

"Higher Education in Modern Mexico," *The Nation's Schools* 35, 6 (June 1945), p. 32.

"Introduction of Dr. Jaime Torres Bodet, Secretary of Education for the Republic of Mexico," in *Mexico's Role in International Intellectual Cooperation* 6, Inter-American Series, Occasional Papers. (Albuquerque, University of New Mexico Press, 1945), p. 51.

"An Editorial from Council 85," *LULAC News,* (February 1946), pp. 5, 15.

"First Regional Conference on the Education of Spanish-Speaking People in the Southwest," *LULAC News,* (February 1946), pp. 12-15.

"Spanish-Speaking People in the United States," in *Information for Speakers,* Race Relations Sunday Packet for February 9, 1947. The Federal Council of Churches of Christ in America, (December 1946), pp. 6-7.

with Virgil E. Strickland, "Spanish Name Spells Discrimination," *The Nation's Schools* 41, (January 1948), pp. 1-7.

"The Default of Leadership," in *Proceedings of the Southwest Council of Education of Spanish-Speaking People* (mimeographed), 4th Regional Conference, (January 1950), pp. 1-7.

"Concerning American Minorities," in *Proceedings of the Southwest Council on Education of Spanish-Speaking People*, 5th Annual Conference, (January 1951), pp. 51-55.

"Education in Latin America," Chapter 3 in *Comparative Education*. A. V. Moehlman and J. S. Roucek, eds. (New York: Dryden Press, 1951), pp. 61-84.

"Education in Mexico," Chapter 4 in *Comparative Education*. A. V. Moehlman and J. S. Roucek, eds. (New York: Dryden Press, 1951), pp. 85-108.

"Mexican Immigrants and Other Spanish Americans," Part of Chapter 6 in *Minorities in American Society*, Charles F. Marden and Gladys Meyer, eds. (New York: American Book Company, 1952, pp. 152-153.

"Spanish-Speaking People in the Southwest: A Brief Historical Review," *California Journal of Elementary Education* 12: 2, (November 1953), pp. 106-111.

"The Crux of the Dual Language Handicap," *New Mexico School Review* 38, (March 1954), pp. 13-15.

"School Integration and Americans of Mexican Descent," *American Unity* 16, 3 (March-April 1958), pp. 9-14.

with Luisa G. T. Sánchez, "Perspective," *Educational Leadership* 15, 8, (May 1958), pp. 464-465.

"Reflections on the Federal Aid Issue," *Texas Observer*, (October 20, 1948), p. 5.

"Cold Devastating Facts," *The Texas Observer*, (August 8, 1959), p. 6.

"Pre-School for All," *The Texas Observer*, (September 4, 1959), p. 7.

"Twice Wounded," *The Texas Observer*, (October 30, 1959), p. 7.

"Problems of Latin Americans," in *Conference on Latin American Relations in the Southwestern United States*. The National Council of the Protestant Episcopal Church, (January 1959), pp. 24-25.

"Quantitative and Objective Criteria in Education: A Delusion," *Texas Journal of Secondary Education* 13, 3, (Spring 1960), PP. 1-5.

"A Pessimistic View," *The Texas Observer*, (December 2, 1960), p. 7.

"A New Frontier Policy for the Americas," *The Alcalde* 19, 7, (March 1961), pp. 9-11.

"The American of Mexican Descent," *The Chicago Jewish Forum* 20, 2 (Winter 1961-1962), pp. 120-124.

"The Latin Citizen: His Hardship, His Promise," *The Texas Observer*, (March 9, 1962), p. 6.

"Proposals on Latins," *The Texas Observer*, (March 16, 1962), p. 7.

"The United Mexican States," Chapter 8 in *Comparative Educational Administration*. Theodore L. Reller and Edgar L. Masphet, eds. (Englewood Cliffs: Prentice Hall, Inc., 1962), pp. 151-165.

"Venezuela," Part of Chapter 18 in *Comparative Educational Administration*. Theodore L. Reller and Edgar L. Mosphet, eds. (Englewood Cliffs: Prentice Hall, Inc., 1962), pp. 375-376.

"A Communication," *The Texas Observer*, (August 23, 1963), pp. 4-5.

"Education in Mexico," Chapter 13 in *The Caribbean: México Today*, A. Curtis Wilgus, ed. (Gainesville: University of Florida Press, 1964), pp. 145-151.

"Past and Present Inter-American Educational Relations: A Personal Memoir," *Inter-American Educational Relations*, Gordon C. Ruscoe, ed. (Los Angeles: University of California, October 8-10, 1964), pp. 1-7.

"Colleges and Democracy," *The Texas Observer*, (May 14, 1965), p. 12.

"The American of Mexican Descent," *The Texas Observer*, (December 31, 1965).

"History, Culture, and Education," in *La Raza: Forgotten Americans*, Julián Samora, ed. (Indiana: University of Notre Dame Press, 1966), pp. 1-26.

"An Educator Speaks Out," *Home Missions* 18, 7 (July 1967), pp. 18-19.

# About the Contributors

ALURISTA was born in Mexico but grew up in California. He now lives in San Diego, where he teaches creative writing and Chicano Literature at San Diego State College. He has been director of the Chicano Studies Center at San Diego State. More than any other poet, he personifies the Movimiento Chicano. Among his works are *Floricanto en aztlán* and *Nationchild Pluma Roja*.

DAVID BALLESTEROS is Dean of the School of Arts and Sciences at the California State University at Sacramento. His fields of specialization include both pedagogy and the humanities.

JOE J. BERNAL formerly was a member of the Texas state senate for Bexar county (San Antonio), where he distinguished himself as an advocate for liberal causes. He is currently executive director of the Commission for Mexican American Affairs of the Archdiocese of San Antonio.

ARTHUR LEON CAMPA is Professor Emeritus in the Department of Foreign Languages and Literatures of the University of Denver. A scholar of wide-ranging interests, he is perhaps best known for his works on the folklore and the history of the Southwest. Among his works is *Spanish Folk-Poetry in New Mexico*.

JESÚS CHAVARRÍA teaches in the Department of History of the University of California at Santa Bárbara. He was one of the implementers of the Plan de Santa Bárbara, the "manifesto" of the academic aspect of the Movimiento Chicano and was for some time director of the Center for Chicano Studies at Santa Bárbara.

ERNESTO GALARZA was born in México and came to the United States during the Revolution, while he was still a young boy. He has seen the life of the Mexican worker at close range and is equally at home in the fields of academe. For many years he has worked for the cause of Chicano labor. Among his best-known works are *Merchants of Labor: The Mexican Bracero Story* and *Barrio Boy*. He now lives in San José, California.

JUAN GÓMEZ-QUIÑONES teaches in the Department of History of the University of California at Los Angeles. He has been active in the creation of the Chicano Studies Center at UCLA and is one of the editors of *Aztlán: International Journal of Chicano Studies Research*. His specialties are Chicano history and labor history; he is the author of *Sembradores: Ricardo Flores Magón y el Partido Liberal Mexicano*.

RICHARD E. LÓPEZ is in the Department of Psychology of the California Polytechnic State University at San Luis Obispo. JULIAN SAMORA is in the Department of Sociology and Anthropology at the University of Notre Dame. He has been involved in the study of Chicano social problems for many years. Among his works are *La Raza: Forgotten Americans* and, with Richard Lamanna, *Mexican-Americans in a Midwest Metropolis: A Study of East Chicago*.

CAREY MCWILLIAMS, editor of *The Nation*, is best known among Mexican Americanists for his book *North from Mexico: The Spanish-Speaking People of the United States*. He was active in the fight against exploitation of agricultural workers and against racial discrimination in California from the 1930s until 1951, when he left the West Coast for New York City to join the staff of *The Nation*.

JAMES NELSON MOWRY is a doctoral student in the Department of Cultural Foundations of Education at the University of Texas, Austin. The title of his dissertation will be "The Educational Thought and Action of Dr. George I. Sánchez."

AMÉRICO PAREDES is in the departments of English and Anthropology at the University of Texas, Austin, where he organized a Mexican American Studies program.

PAUL S. TAYLOR is Professor Emeritus in the Department of Economics at the University of California, Berkeley. He was one of the first Anglo scholars to focus on the problem of social and economic discrimination against Mexican Americans. Among his works are *An American-Mexican Frontier: Nueces County, Texas* and the multivolume *Mexican Labor in the United States*.

# Chicano Studies Center Publications

CSC Publications, and other Chicano publishing outlets, were created to provide responsible and reliable sources for materials on Chicanos. Since its inception, CSC Publications has been filling a much needed service by providing diverse quality materials through its various publications. These books are a valuable research and bibliographical resource for teachers at all educational levels and an authoritative and credible information source for the general public. All editorial responsibility rests with the editorial board, which is comprised of concerned scholars in various disciplines who are indigenous to the Chicano community.

## Aztlán-International Journal of Chicano Studies Research

*Aztlán* is a forum for scholarly writings on all aspects of the Chicano community. It is the first journal sponsored by a university or college in the United States that focuses critical discussion and analysis on Chicano matters as they relate to the group and to the total U.S. society. The works presented offer original research and analysis in the social sciences, humanities and the arts, related to Chicanos. ($15.00 Individuals, $20.00 Libraries and Institutions for one volume year/3 issues. Single issue prices available.)

# Aztlán Reprint Series

**The Emergence of El Partido de la Raza Unida: California's New Chicano Party** by Alberto Juárez. This pamphlet examines the recent emergence of La Raza Unida Party in California and Texas basing it in its historical/political context. It also explores the feasibility and required success factors involved in establishing such a party in light of the "rise and fall" tradition of third parties in U.S. political history. (Reprint from Aztlán, Vol. 3, No. 2, 28 pp., $.75)

**The First Steps: Chicano Labor Conflict and Organizing 1900-1920** by Juan Gómez-Quiñones. The author discusses Chicano Labor organizing during the period 1900-1920 based on published information and archival material, government publications, newspapers, unpublished materials and numerous secondary sources from Mexico and the United States. The pamphlet provides a profile of Chicano labor, suggestions as to patterns of Chicano activity and indications for possible future research within the context of labor in the U.S., the growth of the U.S., Mexican population at the time, Mexican factors, and labor distribution in the Southwest. (Reprint from Aztlán, Vol. 3, No. 1, 40 pp., $.95)

**The Organizing of Mexicano Agricultural Workers: Imperial Valley and Los Angeles, 1928-34, An Oral History Approach** by Devra Anne Weber. Covers four major labor organizational efforts in agriculture: the 1928, 1930 and 1934 strikes in the Imperial Valley and the 1933 strike in El Monte, near Los Angeles. Utilizing a primary oral history approach with participants of the strikes as well as examining archives, retrospective newspapers, government publications and numerous secondary sources, the author provides an original and innovative contribution to this period's literature. (Reprint from Aztlán, Vol. 3, No. 2, 44 pp., $.95)

**The El Monte Berry Strike of 1933** by Ronald W. López. This article, published in early 1970, was one of the first studies to explore more critically the role of Mexican participation in the agricultural strike of the 1930's. Using interview, government documents, archives and retrospective newspapers, the author profiles the El Monte Berry Strike and helped set the trend in this aspect of Chicano Labor history. (Reprint from Aztlán, Vol. 1, No. 1, 16 pp., $.60)

**Chicano Studies Center Publications**
**405 Hilgard Avenue, Los Angeles, California 90024 U.S.A.**
**(213) 825-2642**

# Chicano Studies Center Publications . . .
## Monograph Series

The Series is intended for longer than journal length articles or studies that cover some aspect of the Chicano experience. The series presents scholarly, original and innovative works that are selected by the Editorial Board both for their quality and their relevance to the Chicano community. Its broad range covers topics in the social sciences, the humanities, the life sciences and the physical sciences.

No. 1—*Mexican American Challenge to a Sacred Cow* by Deluvina Hernández is a critical review and analysis of two major university research studies that attempt to causally relate Chicano "values" with low academic achievement in the public schools. This work is one of the first projects to seriously question the concept of "cultural deprivation" among Chicanos. ($2.50 per copy)

No. 2—*Antología del Saber Popular* es una collección de folklore Mexicano y Chicano. La obra incluye cantares, proverbios, adivinanzas, cuentos, leyendas, fábulas, tradiciones, mitos y otras formas de expresión del pueblo Chicano. "Este conjunto pasa a formar el alma de un pueblo y va a rebasar barreras políticas y obstáculos geográficos, para encontrarse hoy en día como una expresión del saber popular al norte de México," (de la nota por Roberto Sifuentes). ($2.95 per copy)

No. 7—*Chicanos In Higher Education: Status and Issues* by Lopez, Madrid and Macías is a major report and resource document providing latest statistical data on the status of Chicanos in higher education. A timely document which substantiates the need for continuing recruitment efforts to balance the underrepresentation of Chicano students in colleges and Universities in the U.S. ($10.00 per copy).

# Creative Series

La literatura y el arte de un pueblo refleja su corazón, su alma. Para presentar el corazón Chicano la Editorial Aztlán inicia una serie creativa. Esta serie presenta las obras de artistas Chicanos y Chicanas de importancia y influencia en el movimiento Chicano y en el renacimiento cultural Chicano.

No. 1—*floricanto en aztlán* is a collection of Alurista's earliest one hundred poems (1968-1969). Alurista has had a major impact on the Chicano movement through his poetry, symbology and views. His influence demands attention. His symbols del barrio, del chuco, de la Chicana, de la madre, and his interpretations of Aztec and Mexican symbols, are a call to action. His poetry is exuberant, nostalgic, angry, loving. "In his art is said what all our poets are saying: reverence, unity, thought, action." (from the preface by Juan Gómez-Quiñones). *floricanto en aztlán* is filled with an excitement and vitality that is testimony to the altering dynamism of the Chicano movement. The book is beautifully illustrated with sixteen original linoleum cuts prepared by Judith Elena Hernández. ($13.50 cloth and $8.95 paper)

No. 2—*The Gypsy Wagon—Un Sancocho de Cuentos Sobre la Experiencia Chicana,* compiled and edited by Armando Rafael Rodríguez, is an anthology of Chicano short stories. The writers lucidly and vividly portray the experiences of the barrio and the life of the Chicano as reflected by the variety of situations, places and thoughts, in which he has found and presently finds himself. The stories range in style and content and are valuable insights to the Chicano existence. ($3.95 paper)

No. 4—*HechizoSpells* is a powerful collection of prose and poems created to review "The global push for human liberation; sensing the hurt in our barrios . . ." The work is comprised of personal "notes on the human condition," followed by a selection of 93 poems, and a brief section in which the author dedicates seven poems. This is the latest and most extensive work of a well-known Chicano poet. A necessary item for all scholars, students, and libraries. This first limited deluxe edition is complemented with original illustrations and designs by Willie Herrón. Truly a collector's item. ($16.95 paper)

# FURIA Y MUERTE: LOS BANDIDOS CHICANOS

**Edited by Pedro Castillo and Alberto Camarillo**

"As Chicano historians write the history of their people, the image of the Mexican 'bandit' must be re-examined. Therefore, a new perspective on Chicano outlawry is needed — the Chicano social bandit."
(from the Introduction).

The editors of this monograph re-examine the historical roles of five "Mexican Bandits," and provide a new and insightful perspective on these figures as Chicano social bandits. The figures presented are: Tiburcio Vásquez, Joaquín Murieta, Elfego Baca, Juan Cortina and Gregorio Cortez.
($1.75 paper)

**Monograph No. 4**